A DISTANT HEARTBEAT

"Eunice Lipton's *A Distant Heartbeat* is an intriguing memoir about an uncle she never met, set within the much broader context of the international brigades who fought against Fascism in the Spanish Civil War. A well-told tale of idealism, diaspora, and both personal and political heartbreak, it draws the reader into the author's lively (and dysfunctional) immigrant family until Uncle Dave's fate resonates with us too."

—LUCY R. LIPPARD, author of
Undermining: A Wild Ride Through Land Use,
Politics, and Art in the Changing West

"A beautifully conceived quest-driven family memoir subtly intertwined with a cultural and political history of Jewish-immigrant New York City in the decades preceding World War II. Given its stylistic clarity, vivid approach, and its 'detective story' qualities, readers will be unable to put it down."

—LEO SPITZER, author of
Hotel Bolivia: The Culture of Memory in a Refuge from Nazism

"Eunice Lipton goes beyond memoir to explore the subliminal legacies of a traumatic event, showing how history survives almost invisibly to affect future generations. Like a jeweler turning a stone, she reveals various facets of a family story that illuminates both past and present."

—PETER N. CARROLL, author of
From Guernica to Human Rights: Essays on the Spanish Civil War

"*A Distant Heartbeat* is a deeply moving, impeccably written homage to an uncle who fought and died in the Spanish Civil War. But in addition to an intimate portrait of an idealistic young man and the Jewish immigrant world that created him, Lipton also asks a question as pertinent today as it was when her uncle Dave joined the Abraham Lincoln Brigade. Why is one brother willing to die for an idea, while another brother thinks it is a wasted life?"

—JILL CIMENT, author of *Act of God*

A DISTANT HEARTBEAT

A War, a Disappearance, and a Family's Secrets

EUNICE LIPTON

University of New Mexico Press ▲ Albuquerque

Printed in the United States of America
21 20 19 18 17 16   1 2 3 4 5 6

Library of Congress Cataloging-in-Publication Data
Lipton, Eunice.
  A distant heartbeat : a war, a disappearance, and a family's secrets / Eunice Lipton.
    pages cm
  Includes bibliographical references.
  ISBN 978-0-8263-5658-1 (pbk. : alk. paper) — ISBN 978-0-8263-5659-8 (electronic)
    1. Lipton, Dave, approximately 1916–1938. 2. Spain—History—Civil War, 1936–1939—
Participation, American. 3. Spain. Ejército Popular de la República. Brigada Internacional,
XV—Biography. 4. Communists—New York (State)—New York—Biography. 5. Young
Communist League of the U.S—Biography. 6. Soldiers—Spain—Biography. 7. Lipton,
Eunice—Family. 8. Jews—New York (State)—New York—Biography. 9. Jewish families—
New York (State)—New York. 10. Bronx (New York, N.Y.)—Biography. I. Title.
  DP269.47.A46L56 2016
  946.081'4—dc23
  [B]

                              2015020397

Cover photographs courtesy of Eunice Lipton
Author photo by Ed Alcock / Agence Myop 2015
Designed by Felicia Cedillos
Composed in Bembo 10.75/14.5

Unless otherwise indicated, all photographs are courtesy of the author.

Contents

Preface

A Distant Heartbeat is a family memoir, a detective story, and an account of a slice of American history banished from textbooks. The story here is of immigrant Left youth politics in New York in the 1930s, seen from the vantage point of a particular Jewish family. At the book's center lie a terrible secret and a breathtaking betrayal, whose traces will not only litter a family's daily life for generations but will also leave their mark on a nation's moral fiber.

I wrote this book as an homage to a brave and elusive uncle and to a decade in New York history, the 1930s, that I wished I had lived through, a period that produced the muscle and optimism to fight for civil rights and, later, the rights of women and gays. At the end of that decade, some 2,800 passionate Americans marched off to fight Fascism in Spain. They became the justly celebrated and unjustly maligned Abraham Lincoln Brigade, a part of the international forces, forty thousand strong in all, that rushed to democratic Spain's defense.

I will share with the reader the pathos and joys of young leftists growing up in the 1930s both through the interplay of one young man—my uncle, Dave Lipton—and his parents, friends, and comrades, and through scenarios lived out on the streets of New York and Paris and in the hills, fields, gullies, and mountains of Spain. To a great extent, the narrative is based on oral histories I recorded from people who lived this history as well as their e-mails and letters to me. Where I fabricate events and dialogue, I have attempted to make the hypothetical dimension absolutely clear to the reader.

A driving question for me has been: Why did some take the unusual step of living their political outrage, as well as their optimism, far from home in a seething, war-torn country, while most did not? I try to understand what might have inspired or inhibited them in their ambitious desire to do nothing less than save Spain from Fascism, and, ultimately, to stop Hitler.

HOW DO WE KNOW WHO THEY WERE?

EACH OF THEM tried to imagine where Dave was shot. They were told that it was up near Gandesa in the mountains of northeastern Spain. Some stared into small black-and-white photographs. They scanned the crushed stones and spiky brush. Others thought they could hear the dull bursts of old Russian guns or feel the heat and thirst, the fear and boredom. They tried everything. But all they got was silence. No one knew anything for sure. Only that one day in May 1938, Dave boarded a ship to France without telling his parents or brothers, that he disappeared into the Spanish Civil War.

I wish I could give you a glimpse of Dave, my uncle, as I knew him, his gait as he strolled Tremont Avenue in the Bronx, the turmoil behind his hesitant smile, his rapt attention in conversation. But I didn't know him, never laid eyes on him. I hadn't been born yet on August 20, 1938, when a sniper shot him dead in Spain. The tricky part, though, was that I thought I knew him. All the whispering and veiled looks, the photographs, the not-quite-indifferent shrugs nagged at me. My uncle Phil, the oldest of his brothers; my father, the second oldest; my mother; later friends and comrades—everyone had a position, an attitude. Some showed shyness and hesitancy, what might have been called their humble respect, others irritation, maybe disappointment. Dave's letters and childish notebooks, bus schedules and theater playbills turned up. Also maps of cities, towns, and battlefields where he had stepped, where he is said to have vanished. The family knew he went to meetings and study groups, organized demonstrations, was earnest and committed. He came from a long line of European leftists; this was especially true of his mother's brothers. But Dave was a good son. He wouldn't just leave like that. A good kid doesn't do that. What got into him?

He lived where we did, where, figuratively, we still do, but as a phantom, a fluttering trace of contradictory memories and emotions: someone slipped his picture in among others, a brother gave a child his name, a severe glance smothered a sarcastic quip. You knew he was there—his wavy blond hair, his dark-brown eyes, his earnest face and winsome smile. In our home, sorrow and rage clung to him.

There's a photograph of Dave in a study group. He sits with five other boys and girls between seventeen and nineteen years old, the girls in sober skirts and starched blouses, the boys in shirts and ties and cardigans. Only Dave is in a suit and tie. They've probably been reading Marx. Maybe they'll become intellectuals, teachers, labor organizers. One or two might dream big and fantasize about the Soviet Union.

Dave spoke several languages. He might study literature or history, diplomacy or law. I heard he was an excellent soccer player and occasional tennis partner, a graceful athlete who could, I suppose, have been fortifying himself for war, but more likely was letting off adolescent steam, grooming himself for admiring eyes.

He was sought out as a friend. I found letters written to him in his late teen years and early twenties. During the summer, there were notes about dances at hotels in the Catskills, where kids went with their parents or worked as camp counselors and waiters. There were references to horseback riding and sneaking milk and cookies in

off-limits hotel kitchens. In fall and winter, those same youngsters wrote to each other about college courses they might take in the years to come or photographs they forgot to give to or get from one another after Labor Day, when autumn leaves drove their daydreams elsewhere. Some inquired shyly, others with bluster, but all were looking for affection and approval. One can still hear the whispering.

Dave's was a life that could have gone almost anywhere. He was a man with the inexhaustible energy that young immigrants carried to America. The aeolian winds held tight only until the ships hit land, and then, even if these new arrivals had to pass through the trials of Ellis Island, those winds blew them into their futures. Dave's family—two brothers and his parents—wrapped him, the youngest, in the soft cotton twills and cozy wools of their love for him. That warmth must have comforted him.

Money was tight, but the family managed. In the late 1920s, when they came to America from Latvia, they'd brought jewelry and cash as well as business know-how from their upscale grocery store in Riga. Grandpa had expert artisanal skills as well, having been a tinsmith as a young man. He married up, Grandma down, both of them for love. Dave seemed fine, safe, ready to live life as an American. And it was New York. The sun shone, comrades were to be had, plus you could slip off to the Catskills for country breezes and deep-green firs. And girls. Life was large. Yet he chose something else—he chose guns, an ocean liner back to the old country, Spain.

Whenever Dave's name was mentioned, Uncle Phil shifted in his seat, Dad's face hardened, Mom's eyes filled with tears. Phil said, "Of the three of us brothers, Dave is the only one that mattered. His life. His death. The rest of us are nobodies. Dave died for something. He was something." Louis, my father, three years younger than Phil, jittery and distracted, interrupted, "Listen, I couldn't find anything wrong with him, that's why I loved him, because there's nobody like that. He was very sweet. I loved him dearly." But then he added, "*Ach*, he died for nothing."

Which was it? Who was this boy? The mild-mannered, determined youngster whose life was thick with bravery and hope? Or a sweet, naïve boy who incoherently threw his life away and permanently deprived his family of their deepest consolation, their youngest son?

My father's "ach, he died for nothing" was a mantra recited automatically whenever someone mentioned Dave. As I grew older, each time I heard those words, that frozen script, it irked me—just as when he repeatedly asked, also in rehearsed phrases, about my mother long after he'd left her for another woman. There was one intermittent event, though, that interrupted the predictability of my father's recitation about Dave. Without warning, on one of those rare evenings when he was home, he would rummage in his closet in the hallway and, reaching to the back of a high shelf, he'd lift out an old shoebox. He would stare at it for a while and then put it away. Once, he said, "Someday, maybe I'll tell you about my brother Dave."

Dave beckoned, a boy trailing danger and sweetness, a pink and pearly streak across a lowing sky. If only he could have been a protective deity, a saint for us. Our family could have used that. But he wasn't. The aura that bathed him gold, edged in black, writhed upward and hardened into shards, falling sharply to earth and penetrating each of us. *Trespass at your own risk* was the notice tacked to his name. One thing was clear, however. In our house, my father owned Dave's story. The only way to Dave was through him and that shoebox.

It's impossible to know how you learn things as a child, why some experiences stay with you while others don't. Despite the claims of psychoanalysis, the track from yesterday to today is unknowable. Time past—coursing, wriggling, flowing upstream into the future— arrives mapless, bulging with the detritus of its trip, junk and glitter alike. One does believe in history, though, and some of us in psycho-analysis. My dad was attached to Dave. That much was clear. And I was attached to my father.

A friend recently told me that she thinks a parent selects a certain one of his or her children to be the carrier—sometimes the healer—of a particular psychic wound the parent has. My friend's mother had chosen her to remember the mother's younger brother, who was taken from her arms as the two were pushed into a cattle car destined for Auschwitz. A guard had yanked her three-year-old brother away from the ten-year-old girl. The girl searched for her brother all her life, and when she gave birth to my friend, her firstborn, she lost all feeling in the hands with which she now would have held her own child, as if her hands would always be reserved for the brother she lost.

My father singled me out. "You're just like me, *meydeleh*," darling, sweetheart, he'd say. He encouraged my restlessness, my attraction to Russian literature and music, an impulse to dance at the slightest hint of a driving beat. He baited my curiosity about his brother. These strands of his love and possessiveness carried desires my father could not possibly know. As he chose me to remember his brother Dave, unbeknownst to him, he also chose me to uncover the nasty chain of events that had led to his own appalling act of betrayal.

Louis—pronounced French style, as in *Louie*—was an impatient man who flitted from job to job. He was like a lot of immigrants in that way; he took work where he could. He painted apartments, sold fruit on the street, flipped hamburgers, drove a cab, sold vacuum cleaners and jewelry door to door. But he also had plain old *spilkes*—ants in his pants. He would hop in his car with some pals and head up to the Catskills, or down to Miami, or out to the boardwalk in Brooklyn. If he had a hankering for a hot dog, he'd drive for hours to get exactly the one he wanted. Women, I am told, relieved his anxiety too.

My father's silence about Dave—with the exception of those ritualized phrases—was all the more striking because words were my father's métier. He was a born salesman. He adored conversation, the to-ing and fro-ing of it, although he maneuvered every which way to grab center stage while at the same time dying for you to take it back, get his dander up, compete with him. He loved that. You could feel how it turned him on. But if your attention wavered when he was in the heat of a story, rage gusted up along his edges, and you didn't know what hit you: "What, you're not listening? You have something better to do?!" Still, and despite the fury, you jumped in and joined the feverish whirl. Unless you were brilliantly strategic in your performance, though, he got bored and wandered off. You worked hard to keep his interest, and when you did, my God, what ecstasy. My father was, as they say, "a piece of work."

Being a writer was the highest of achievements in my father's mind, and it turned out to be a clue to what was in that shoebox in the closet. "I write at night, but then I tear it up," he said. He was a serious letter writer, using many romantic flourishes in his phrasing and highly worked handwriting. He wrote about where he was living at the moment, how he felt. Sometimes he would tell you about something he was reading. He responded to questions you had asked or things you'd said in your last communication. "Dear Eunice," he wrote to me when I was nineteen and traveling in Europe, "I received your 'Mr. Lipton, Where Are You?' card, a few days ago. I got a great kick out of it. No, dear, I haven't given up on you. I love you and miss you as ever."

Wherever my father lived, his favorite spot was the table where he wrote his letters. That's where the gates to his own private paradise swung open, and he would smile and write and dream about being a wise and good man, generous and kind and even brave. It's so odd—or was it just in the cards?—that letters would be my father's downfall.

Now that my parents are gone, I find myself wondering more about Dave, as if their deaths unlocked a no-entry zone. Perhaps it's the mysteriousness of the trajectory of Dave's life that continues to baffle me, or the way he hovered over us and continues to, both there and not there at the same time. Perhaps I am free to think about him now, because although I see my mother and father near him, they no longer demand anything of me. Nor do I have to confront them with what I find. Dave belongs to the family. He has infiltrated all of our beings. He also belongs to American and European history, a young warrior whose idealism remains a driving urge in all democracies. You see it in people who volunteer to fight diseases in foreign countries, who go to the Middle East and implicate themselves in the war between Arabs and Israelis. I can picture Dave and his comrades among those involved in the fight against global capitalism, alongside the kids in Occupy Wall Street demonstrations, in the crowds confronting the murderous impulses of urban police forces toward unarmed African American men and women.

There are things I'd like to ask my uncle, things I'd like to know about from his point of view. Why, for example, did my father refer to him with such a mixture of disdain and sadness? Why did my mother cry at the mention of his name? What made him, at twenty-two, pick up and go to Spain?

I'd like to know, after all is said and done, whether he believes that idealism is a worthy guide in life, whether there are principles worth dying for. Dying. What did he know back then about life and death, when he was yet a boy? He could know nothing about what it means to be extinguished. But maybe that's why he was able to go to Spain on such a journey—because he knew nothing of it. He was too young to comprehend never seeing his mother and father again, never touching his girlfriend again. Did he even have a girlfriend? But might not he have thought, considerate person that he was supposed to have been, what it would be like for his parents never to see *him* again?

Idealism blew Dave back across the sea to Europe, where he was born. Surely leaving for Spain was just a longing that overtook him, and he consented: "Yes, I'll do that," he said to himself. "I can do that." Yet I sense otherwise. His leaving, or rather the memory of it left behind in my family, carries thicker sediment. The references to Dave are too skittish to suggest a simple tale of youthful heroism.

For a good part of my life, I was an art historian, so you would think I'd know how to analyze and represent the past. Yet searching for Dave, fixed as he is in my father's orbit, intimidates me. First of all, I would have to separate the two, and it was doubtful if that could be done completely. Then, I knew my father, and I didn't know Dave. Normally the lack of firsthand knowledge would not be a handicap. I never would have written about people or events in the past if it had been. My father's personality, however, and, more important, his place in my life *as* my father could be a larger problem.

What more, though, do I know of Louis, after all, than what I can learn about my uncle? Yes, I have the pieces I collected from my father over the years, the ones I picked up willingly, the others that flew into me when I wasn't looking. But is that my *father*? Don't I have as much dependable information about Dave—photographs and letters, people's memories, the stories and confidences his friends and comrades put in my hands? If each photo is ipso facto someone else's view of him and not him exactly, precisely, definitively, it nonetheless is evidence of something. As are anecdotes. They may be other people's constructions, but they result from a bond between Dave and another person. And Dave's letters are certainly him. As are the playbills and bus schedules he stored away. Then there are the things his parents saved and my father gathered together: his diploma from George Washington High School, a certificate from a metal workshop, his notebooks in Yiddish from Riga, where he was born, his document of American citizenship.

What determines what is true about a person, an event, an object from the past? What constitutes knowledge and truth? Deciphering, knowing, remembering, forgetting. We know some things and not others. We think we know some things and we don't, and perhaps too, we think we don't know things and we do. As a psychoanalyst once said to me when I apologized for the imprecision of a certain memory, "Whatever you remember is true."

After reading Dave's letters home from Spain, traveling to places he'd been, and talking to his friends and family, I began to witness the unfolding of an unexpected landscape. There are certainly more "facts" about Dave and more personal projections about Louis. But one side isn't as completely empirical as it seems, and the other is not as swamped in psychological morass. There's a little of both in each: some fact and some muddle, and loads of interpretation.

As I searched for my uncle, I relished old New York vistas, trying to imagine them as Dave saw them. Elevated subway trains, cafeterias, Jewish delis. I hiked the parched hills of northeastern Spain and

thirties. Everyone says the college was on fire then. The children of largely Jewish immigrants from eastern Europe only had to open their mouths for some form of Marxism to fall out. Of course, they talked mostly to each other. Socialists and Communists detested each other and argued with icy wit and snide repartee. The most savage exchanges were between Stalinist and anti-Stalinist Communists, in particular, Trotskyites. You could say that they turned the fervor of traditional Talmudic study—commentary on the Bible—into equally fervent political critique.

Young intellectuals like Irving Howe, Alfred Kazin, Daniel Bell, Nathan Glazer, and Irving Kristol hurled insults at each other from different alcoves of the City College cafeteria, while other students at City, whose names most people don't know today, organized the homeless and the unemployed, worked for the labor movement, and left for Spain. Edwin Rolfe, a poet, went, as did Abe Osheroff, an activist and later a filmmaker; factory workers and athletes, like Irving Weissman and Max Shufer respectively, also left. Among the City College students who died in Spain were Wilfred Mendelson, Leon Sloan Torgoff, Leo Grachow, Harry Perlman, and Dave Lipton.

When I arrived at City, few kids consciously carried their family's leftist history with them. Most of us were mesmerized by Freudian psychoanalysis and Sartrean existentialism, with Dostoyevsky and Nietzsche thrown in. I remember the morning when a hush fell over our medieval history class, when a bleary-eyed, voluptuous girl named Susan stumbled into the classroom clutching *The Idiot*. Everyone knew she'd stayed up all night reading it. (But how in the world could she have read that many pages in one night? I said to myself.)

Joseph McCarthy's rabid anti-Communism threw an anesthetizing cloth across our late 1950s, as did the memory of the electrocuted Julius and Ethel Rosenberg in their brutish coffins, front-page pictures of them seared into our brains. We never mentioned the Holocaust, but it drenched our intellectual and emotional lives, just as it poisons Asa Leventhal in Saul Bellow's *The Victim* as, heart pounding and out of breath, he convinces himself that a malcontent Christian coworker is hounding him down the streets of New York in the scorching summer heat. Because he is a Jew.

City College of the thirties had been alive with hope, but in the fifties, we were scared. We became ardent intellectuals, and frankly, that served us well. My father had no patience for the politics of City in the thirties: "My brother? He was stupid. Look at those guys who came back from Spain. They're millionaires. Some Communists!"

That's where the Spanish Civil War went in my archive: the slot called "Died for Nothing." *But* with the caveat that my father would never forget his brother. No one visited our lives more than that brother.

When I started going to Europe at nineteen, I never went to Spain, where the Fascist general Francisco Franco was dictator until he died in 1975. When asked why I didn't go, I'd say that I had an uncle who died there in the Civil War. But maybe that was bragging: I may appear to be a depressed, Dostoyevsky-reading girl, but we did stuff in my family, we believed in things.

So when *Land and Freedom* was released in 1995, when I was middleaged, I went to see it out of curiosity.

The film is a conventional adventure story. Or rather, that's its trick as it draws you into what, for many people, is one of the most inspiring and heartbreaking moments of the twentieth century, the Spanish Civil War. The hero, an English Communist coincidentally named David, hears a rousing speech in Liverpool in the spring of 1936, about the plight of the Spanish Republic. He decides to go to Spain.

Forty thousand men and women from all over the world did the same between 1936 and 1938. Politically astute people everywhere knew that the Fascist coup in Spain against the legally elected leftist government was the first organized showdown between the Left and Right in Europe. Mussolini and Hitler maneuvered politically into their positions in Italy and Germany in the twenties and thirties, but in

Spain—medieval, Catholic, normally sleepy twentieth-century Spain—civil war exploded. Wildly unequal sides faced off, with the Italians and Germans sending arms, planes, and soldiers to the Fascists, while the rest of Europe and America stood by, feigning neutrality.

After the meeting in London, we next see David driving in the parched Spanish countryside with other volunteers. When their truck stops, they jump out, young and eager, and are introduced to the local militia unit, which is Trotskyite and represents the POUM, the Partido Obrero de Unificación Marxista (Workers' Party of Marxist Unification). The new recruits adjust their ears and eyes, their bodies to the intense, dry heat, the new faces and languages, the fear, and the excitement.

David is a good man, fair and amiable, open hearted and brave. He is a comrade. He meets and falls in love with Blanca, who, it turns out, is an anarchist. As Loach told an interviewer, "We wanted to reflect the confusion of the time and all the varied personal stories, because a lot of it was haphazard and people ended up fighting along with others for merely accidental reasons. It all happened in a great hurry where everyone rushed off to the front."

David, a Communist, becomes convinced that the POUM militia is undermining Communist strategies. He leaves Blanca and his new friends and goes to Barcelona. There, he observes, as George Orwell famously did in *Homage to Catalonia*, the Communists sabotaging the Left, inciting dissension and betrayal. Philosophical and political conflicts between Trotskyites and Communists were insoluble, their mutual hatred fatal. Just as the Soviet Union was holding its purge trials (and Stalin had ordered the murder of Trotsky in Mexico City), in Spain, the Communists destroyed those who disagreed with them. The Fascists won, changing the course of the twentieth century. The Soviets played their nasty part in that.

After his experience in Barcelona, David turns back into the Spanish landscape in search of the militia—and Blanca—and finds them. But, some weeks afterward, members of the group are confronted by a Communist envoy of troupes sent to rid the area of unruly Trotskyite and anarchist militias. As the troupes open fire on the band, Blanca throws herself in front of a wounded comrade and is shot dead midstep. The camera doesn't look at David.

Next we are at David's funeral in England, fifty years later. At the graveside, his granddaughter, a robust girl with thick dark hair, haltingly offers a eulogy. She is not used to calling attention to herself. From her large, worn purse, she removes a bulging, faded red neckerchief. She steps forward to the grave. She unties the scarf and empties what we know is the soil of Spain onto her grandpa's coffin. The men and women at the grave raise their fists in the Popular Front salute. Their passion, their tenderness, their attachment to each other, and their idealism sustained over the years unhinge me. Side by side at their friend's funeral, they salute David and their own ancient hopes and disappointments, as well as their abiding stubbornness and faith. They were not destroyed by what happened in Spain. As in that famous song "I Dreamed I Saw Joe Hill Last Night," about the union organizer executed by firing squad in Utah in 1915, their comrades in Spain never died. For these believers, there was something in them that could not be killed.

Leaving the movie theater, I begin to tell my husband, Ken, about my uncle. We walk home, a mile up Broadway, and I can't stop talking. The stories tumble out. It begins, I tell him, when I am thirteen and up in the Catskills, at my grandparents' rooming house, with my parents and brother, my cousins, their parents, and my father's aunts and uncles and their children. It is the week of Passover. On a rainy day, a bunch of the younger cousins entertain ourselves in one of the top-floor bedrooms.

After a game of Monopoly, we flop around restlessly on the three beds—there are always several in each room. My grandparents rent to families traveling long distances who can't afford normal hotels and sleep three or four to a room. My eye wanders to a dresser with a large curving mirror. Photos cover the top, some of Grandma and Grandpa when they were young, some of older people, maybe their parents, and some of their three sons. In one, the three boys are together, perhaps at a wedding. I must have seen this before, because I recognize them, Dave with his wavy, almost marcelled blond hair next to the darker-complected Louis and Phil.

I get off the bed and go over to the dresser. I open and shut the top drawers—a deck of cards, some thread, safety pins. I bend down and start fiddling with the large bottom drawer, which is stuck. My cousin Jerry, who is fifteen, kneels down next to me. I yank and shake the drawer, pull and push it until it jumps forward into my hands. An old-time smell leaps out. A shoebox sits at the bottom.

"Sh-shut it now," my seven-year-old brother, David, stammers, turning toward the windows. Jerry, Debby—my uncle Phil's daughter, who is six—and I sit staring into the drawer. My brother wanders back and looks too. The box waits, mute, its pistachio-green color like the interior of an old upholstered railway car you'd find in an Edward Hopper painting. I pick it up and put it on my lap. I hesitate for a split second, and then I lift the cover.

Piled one atop the other, reaching halfway up the box, are letters and photographs lying gently in cellophane sleeves, the lot of them glowing yellow white like a winter sun. When I pluck out a little red, white, and blue pin with a tiny dangling Liberty Bell and the year 1939 etched across it, something thuds to the bottom. A harmonica.

"L-look at that big picture." David nudges me. I ease out a 9" x 11" black-and-white photograph. It's of a group of men in berets and soldiers' hats sitting and lying under a tree on what appears to be a warm summer's day.

"That's Dave," Debby says, pointing to our fathers' brother, who is on the right, bareheaded, with a sprig of flowers tucked behind his

ear, his eyes narrowed against the sun. He sits between two men wearing berets. Only the flower makes him remarkable. Dave gazes at us, his legs pulled up, his elbows wrapped around them.

"This is n-nice," my brother says, fingering the photo. "I have his name." I turn the box's contents onto the bed.

"Soccer," Jerry says, picking up a photograph of a sports team posing together. The photo is dated 1931. Our uncle is a young teenager. He smiles foolishly, as if he's just stopped himself from laughing. He's a boy, his naked legs shy. He has paid no special attention to his wavy hair, which wriggles out around his head like the locks of Medusa.

"My father used to play soccer," I say.

"Your father used to do everything. According to him, anyway," says Jerry. Then he picks up several very small pictures taken about seven years after the soccer photo. They are little black-and-white

shots of Dave from midtorso up, the type of pictures you take for passports today and that were, at the time, taken in photo booths in subway stations, mementos of friendship or love. In two of them, Dave wears a dark-colored boatneck sweater over a work shirt open at the throat. On top is a coarse overcoat. He's a student revolutionary. In one of those photos, he gazes downward and to the side, his lids heavy, his expression pensive. In the other, he stares out knowingly, wistfully, too wise for such a young person. It's a performance, a young man playing a role. He kept the pictures, a reminder of something. Eugène Delacroix painted a boy like him in *Liberty Leading the People*, but Delacroix's student is dressed in a vest and frock coat, disheveled scarf, and top hat.

"He's so dashing," I say to Jerry.

"Yeah," says Jerry, "but look at him in these with another guy. They're like Siamese twins."

It's true, they must have been good friends. Dave is wearing a suit and tie and the same overcoat as before, which now seems soft and elegant. In one picture, he leans his head into his friend's, touching him lightly. His expression is somber, a little mistrustful, but his friend smiles contentedly. Perhaps he knows Dave well enough to see that his friend is only trying on severity, that underneath, he is forgiving and sweet and worried. In another, Dave's solemnity crumples into uncontrollable giggles. His companion laughs too.

There's another photo of him as a soldier, but ghostly and thread-bare, a skinny, nervous man whose clothes hang indifferently on him, all pockets, buttons, and sleeves. I put it at the bottom of the pile. Next we're all scanning a picture of Dave crawling on a rocky, barren hill. On the back of it are the words "Sierra Pandols, Hill 666." At first glance, Dave seems alone, examining something closely on the ground, but little by little, other soldiers' caps begin to dot the horizon, popping up between low brush and rocks. There are no trenches, no cavities in the earth at all, not a single place to hide.

Maybe these pictures are from World War II. We don't know. Then we look again at the large photo with all the men beneath the tree. Our uncle, like the rest, seems tense. Written in the corner is the date, July 1938. I pick up some letters, but they're in Yiddish.

"We better put everything away," I say. "And not tell anyone. Okay?" I close the box and put it back in the drawer. I turn away from the others, hoping they'll leave, which they do, banging down the stairs toward the aroma of roasting chicken.

My grandparents' house in Hurleyville, the Flower House, where they lived and earned a living, is in my memory like a stage set where life happened, beyond which something else, other people's lives, passed grayly by, or didn't happen at all. The house was a beautiful, serene place, tall and white, with a red roof, red window frames, and a long wraparound porch. Its three stories piled evenly one on the other, and the whole of it stretched right up to the sky, like a lofty white bird with red markings. Its porch was open, almost outside, and when the storms came in August, you had to go inside. Otherwise, it was a porch for musing, a place where children played their secret games, where adults lingered, daydreaming, reading mystery stories, or gazing up at drenched and sprawling pine and maple trees.

It was a house where you could travel unpredictably from one world to another—there was enough space for that, and few rules to stop you. You'd be packing your doll into her carriage when your grandfather, out of the blue, offered you a seat next to him at his worktable in the garage, and the world turned upside down as you crossed the threshold into a shimmering hearth of a room, where men made things. Or you'd be playing pickup sticks, and strains of Grandma's favorite melody from *Carmen* would fill the house. You'd stretch like a kitten, forgetting your game.

As I look back on Hurleyville, perhaps it was the optimism embedded in childhood that made it so sweet, the vividness and dependability of each moment as it rolled into the next, continuing down the years. That life, saturated in colors, smells, sounds, and light, was so fresh and so surprising that it tasted like freedom itself, the nourishment of a lifetime that would endlessly replenish. It would always be paradise.

But this was also a house where a mother and father lived who had lost four sons. Of their six boys, four were dead.

A half hour after we finish examining the box upstairs, everyone gathers for Passover dinner. There are no prayers or discussions of the holiday. We kids have no idea why the day is special, except that it is an occasion to get together. None of the children has ever been to a synagogue. The adults speak to each other in a mixture of Yiddish and English.

It is my father's family here in the house. At the table are Phil and his wife, Mona, and my cousin Debby. Also Grandma's brother, Lazar, his sons, Jacky and Benny, and his wife, Yadasha, who periodically disappears into the Soviet Union and then quietly returns, bringing news to those who want it. There is Grandma's delicate younger sister Emma, who will soon be dead of throat cancer. And her affectionate husband, Solomon, the upholsterer with the thick, straight black hair and nasty facial warts, and their two children, Shirley and another Jacky. There is Grandma's other sister, Rose, with her handsome husband, Robert, and my cousin Jerry, their adopted son. Everyone calls Rose a whore behind her back. She wears low-cut blouses, throws her honey-colored hair around, and has a particularly emphatic way of smoking, as if her cigarette were in a holder. She's a sort of Latvian Joan Crawford. Then there are my mother and father, my brother and me.

My father sits at the table relaxed, smiling to himself. His gabardine shirt falls softly along his shoulders and arms, open at the neck. His little mustache is just so. After the gefilte fish and chicken soup with matzo balls, the conversation idles, and I watch him scan the table restlessly until he lands on Mona.

"Mona," he says. "Reading any interesting books?"

"Not really, Louis. I'm not much of a reader." She has a heavy Hungarian accent. "I'm a *balabuster*," she adds—she means that she's a good cook and housekeeper—eyeing my mother, who works as a bookkeeper.

"Oh, is that right? What do you do when Phil brings his doctor friends home?"

"I serve them a good meal," she says proudly, looking at her husband. He looks away. You know he hates her. Phil is a sorry type, a man who sleeps with prostitutes because the merest hint of rejection mortifies him. He couldn't be bothered having conversations with women, listening, responding, taking the time. He'd wanted the social niche that required a wife, but when he married, the intimacy nauseated him.

"That's it, Monalah? You don't converse with them?"

Little Debby sits like a block of stone in her chair, staring ahead.

When the chicken reaches the table, my father digs in, forgetting Mona. He's satisfied with himself. Phil hates Mona, and Louis hates Phil. Any way to get at his brother is a good way. He once told me, "We weren't close until we went to America, just the two of us on the boat. Then we got a little closer. He became sick. He caught a bad cold, got inflammation of the eyes, and then I started having feelings toward him. But afterward, I disliked him again." The relationship never sweetened. Near the end of their lives, my father visited Phil and his second wife in La Jolla, California. The two brothers weren't getting along. One day Phil, the doctor, screamed at my father, who was awaiting brain scan results: "I hope you have brain cancer!"

"So, how's business, Louis? You gonna make a go of this one?" inquires Rose in her gravelly voice.

"Come over sometime, I'll show you, Rosy," he answers, winking and chewing at the same time.

"You can't go down to Miami at the drop of a hat anymore, chasing . . ." She stops in midsentence as she notices my mother.

"Sure I can," my father says. "Nothing stops me. I'm my own boss."

"Yeah, some boss," says Robert, Rose's husband. "I hear your partner's not too happy. You'll ruin the luncheonette, like you do everything."

"Oh, is that right, Mr. Successful Fruit Peddler, what has my partner been saying, my brilliant *schnorrer* partner?"

"Never mind."

"What do I care what he says? He's got no balls, that Italian wife of his pushing him around."

Just then, my brother looks up from his plate, where he's been organizing his food into discrete piles, and says, "Where's Uncle Dave?" The words slap the Passover table shut. Mouths clench, eyelids drop. At the sink, Grandma's body stiffens, and she leans forward on her elbows. My father looks nervously toward his mother.

"What a tragedy," Yadasha murmurs.

My mother sags in her seat. "He was the nicest man I ever knew," she says.

My father glares at my brother. "Can't you sit up straight?" he yells. "And what are you staring at, Trudy?" he snaps at my mother.

"Nothing, Louis. Nothing," she murmurs.

"He threw his life away," Louis whispers. "What good was it?" He's yelling now. "What use was it? Somebody want to answer me? A young boy's life, destroyed."

"What good? Are you crazy, Louis?" demands Yadasha, her voice rising too. "If Roosevelt had done what those men and women did and the Soviet Union did, and if America hadn't waited till 1941, we might never have had a war. We might have destroyed Hitler at the start."

"Oh yeah, Yadasha. If you're such a true believer, you send your own sons next time."

"Louis, don't excite yourself," my mother interjects, nervously stretching her hand out to him. He shoves it away.

"Send your own goddamn sons!" my father hollers again.

Grandma straightens up then, smooths her apron, and looks at my father. "*Zayn sha!*"—quiet!—she warns him. "*Genug.*" Enough.

My father tells me that one day in December 1938, he runs down to a pier in Manhattan to meet a ship carrying veterans home from Spain. He knows that his brother's friend Ben Katine will be among the returning men. Katine wrote to him a week earlier, on December 9, telling him as much. Always punctual, my father is especially careful to leave himself plenty of time. He wants to be up front when disembarkation begins. He presses himself forward through the crowd, remembering a bullfight he saw in Havana, tension slicing the air, the unstoppable animal flesh hurtling forward, blood on the ground, on the bull's back, the heaving, the toreador's conniving flirtation. Life. Then death. *La muerte.*

The boys and men surge up and forward out of the ship to their mothers and fathers, their girlfriends and boyfriends, their brothers and sisters. My father is frantic. "Concentrate," he commands himself as his eyes skid from face to face. "Why shouldn't he be here?" he's muttering. "Where is he? Maybe he's in the bathroom. I'm sure he's here, he must be. Why should we believe he's gone? We got no formal notice, just Ben's letter saying so. It could have been hearsay."

But then he recalls Ben's words: "I am sorry to have to be the one to tell you that your brother Dave is dead."

Ben spots my father and rushes over to him, grabbing his arm. "Louis, I'm so sorry, I'm so very sorry."

My father is crying now. "He's not with you, Ben, is he?"

"Louis, you all right? You know. . . . Here, I have something for you." Ben lays his suitcase on the ground amid the thrusting crowd. He opens it and pulls out a small packet of letters and photographs, along with a harmonica. He hands them to my father. "He gave his life for a good cause. Remember that, Lou. I have to go now. I'll be in touch." Ben's girlfriend and parents are waiting nearby. My father stands there, grasping the harmonica in one hand, the little package in the other.

That day, he will have to tell his parents that their son is dead. He takes the subway back to their apartment and packs the mementos Ben brought him into the shoebox we found as children. He adds some letters he has. I don't know who put the box in that bottom drawer in Hurleyville where we fell upon it, but later, when my grandparents became old and ill and forgetful, my father must have taken it home to the Bronx and placed it in the back of his closet. This is the box my brother and I watch him take down over the years, bending over it, almost davening as a Jew praying would. I never see him examine the contents piece by piece. He just holds the box in his hands and then puts it away. The simplicity and repetition of the gesture drops into my memory like a religious act might, a medieval saint holding the instruments of his torture, or the young Mary folded into herself as the angel Gabriel whispers her awful fate. My brother and I observe my father performing this ritual many times. His attention to Dave never fades. It is the only subject that silences him, that draws a bead of concentration out of his habitual anxiety and self-absorption. We can't but notice this, because we always feel that he could walk away from us forever and never look back. He could drive to Florida and forget to return, be furious at us for some fabricated slight and never call or write again. But we know he will never stop loving his brother.

He knows we are watching him, and we know with absolute certainty that this is a declaration: you will never mean as much to me as Dave does.

As we grow up, we have only the vaguest idea that Dave had been a Communist and died in Spain. There is no trace of his brother's leftism in our father. To the contrary, over and over again, he repeats to us, "Nothing is worth dying for. Don't do anything people can hold up in your face. Mind your own business." I have no idea how to reconcile the reverence of his gestures with his contemptuous "he threw his life away."

The day after I see *Land and Freedom*, I call my father. It's been ten years since I've spoken to him. I want to ask him something about his brother. The lapsed years fall away. We were never folks for social niceties, so when he picks up the phone, I say, "Hi, Dad, how are you? Listen, I saw a very interesting film last night. About the Spanish Civil War. You should see it. You'd like it." My father and I had gone to many movies together. We had puzzled over them for hours, dissecting plots and characters.

"I don't go to movies anymore," he says.

"Oh, too bad. You used to love them." Why am I needling him?

"Who needs them?" he tosses back.

"Your brother Dave, he died in Spain, didn't he?"

"Yeah?"

I hear his wife, Lena, in the background. "What does your daughter want now?" she's saying in Yiddish.

"Why did he go, Dad?"

"Oh, he was a sincere left-winger, always helping people, giving out the *Daily Worker*, going to demonstrations. He was a good public speaker too." It's as if we've been sharing intimacies like this without interruption, as if the ten years of silence never happened.

"Where did his politics come from?"

"We all had it, it was in all of us, the whole family. But Dave went to the extreme."

"What do you mean, in all of you? I never thought of you as political. Mom was the political one." My voice is rising. I can see him smiling: you're enjoying this, meydeleh. We are so adept at teasing a tale out of a string of indifferent facts and snaring each other. And here we are again, in the best way we ever had together, in exactly that kind of conversation.

"No, it was my family, believe me," he's saying. "Your mother only came to it when she met Dave. As children, it was in our house. Grandma's brothers were Bolsheviks. Not Lazar in the US, the other ones who stayed in Russia and Riga. They were always coming over and talking to us. That's how we stopped being religious. Plus, Grandma's father, the rebbe, dying. The uncles didn't respect the Sabbath, and we began to do the same. We didn't want to go to cheder anymore anyway. The teachers were old and ignorant. They were great, her brothers, big and handsome, and one of them, Dovid, was sweet as honey. They had so many stories about the Soviet Union, and they brought us books to read, Yiddish books by I. L. Peretz and Sholem Aleichem."

"Your parents were businesspeople. They weren't Communists," I remind him.

"Well, they believed in it, in their hearts, but they had to make a living, didn't they? They were caught. We kids could go on believing. And we did. All of us."

"It sure didn't show."

"You only knew us afterward," he's saying. "When we came to the States, things changed. Phil became an A student, and I, I went my crazy way. Not that I wasn't interested. I went to a Marxist school down by Union Square for a while. But I was young. I wanted to be with girls, have a good time. With Dave, it was something else. It became his life. Who could have predicted it?" My father's voice falters.

I know bits and pieces of all this, but they are like doodads pinned to a hat, ornaments catching the light, baffling the eye. It isn't a narrative that coalesces for me. The family has leaned left with greater or lesser intensity, each person in his or her own way. They have also been driven, some more than others, by specifically American urges: Have a good time. Take care of yourself first and foremost. Compete. Leave politics to others. But now, an electric charge lights up the story, and details leap out and prick my memory and my conscience. And my curiosity.

Young people come to a new land and choose the attire that suits them. One dresses for seduction, another for professional success. The youngest chooses politics—idealism and commitment to social equality, a willingness to separate from family, to court sadness and danger, even to risk life, and to never give up. These were the roads taken by the three brothers: Louis, Phil, Dave, who, by the way, changed their names from Lifshitz to Lipton in the mid-1930s.

What gripped me in Loach's film was the never giving up, the not dying. Maybe there was something, too, about Dave and my father. There was such a stark contrast between the two men. And my father's attachment to his brother was so anomalous, the overworked choreography of taking down that box, bending over it like a mother over a cradle, the sorrow and the emotional display, but also the contempt. It got under my skin.

"Dad, what do you think actually made him go?" I ask. "It was a decision. Plenty of people were anti-Fascist, but they didn't go to Spain."

He's not listening.

"It's difficult for you to understand," he says. "I had my mind set on going, and then I found out that he left. I would have watched over him. You know, in those years, for a youngster like myself, it was hard to get out of a marriage. I didn't want to get married. You should have seen me as a kid. I was tough. I was wild, too—that's true. My mother used to send me out during the war to sell cigarettes and soap to German soldiers. I was seven years old. I did it, I wasn't afraid. And I saw plenty, believe me. Plenty. Ach, I never talk about it. What's the difference? I saw people shot. Sometimes I saw dead people, and soldiers would bash their heads in after they were dead. Just like that. For fun. I saw it. She knew I could handle it. She was proud of me. She showed me off to the family. 'See this *boychik*,' she'd say, 'such a brave boy, our Leipke.' Yeah, brave. They didn't know. Those soldiers were animals. They didn't care I was kid. And what about the corpses hanging from the lampposts? And the women floating dead, face-down in the river? You knew they were Communist because their hair was cut short. After that, I'd run out to the circus in the mornings to watch the executions. They couldn't control me anymore."

"It must have been terrible for you, Dad." I humor him.

"No, it wasn't terrible. That's life, sweetheart. You never know, do you?"

"They were German soldiers?" I'm intrigued now.

"Who else? The country was filled with Germans, especially in the cities, in business. World War I was their opportunity to swallow Latvia whole. It wouldn't have been as bad if they were Russian."

Naturally, my father defends the Russians. But it's not the Soviet Union he's thinking about. It's Dostoyevsky and Tchaikovsky, Gorky and Turgenev.

"What was Dave like as a boy, Dad?"

"Why are you so interested in him? I don't remember. He kept to himself a lot."

"You don't remember?"

"No. My mother and father favored me. My mother used to say I had a *yiddishe kop*. That's why she sent me onto the streets as a boy. And let me come to New York with Phil. It was my idea."

"There was nothing remarkable about Dave, nothing special about him? I thought you loved him."

"David? He had a nice nature. Good-natured, like my father. Very good-natured. He was just one of those easygoing fellas, a good-looking boy, serious. Everybody loved him. It seems that I impressed him very much too."

"Uh-huh. Did you admire him?"

"No."

"Even though he did such a brave, idealistic thing?"

"No. What did I care?"

"So he was an even-tempered guy?"

"Yeah. A little hard to get to, though."

"Well, I don't know, Dad, but I felt really sad watching that Spanish Civil War film."

"You were always emotional," he says.

"Yeah. Well, I'd like to find out more about him."

"What's to find out? He's dead. That's it. There's nothing to find out. He was a good boy. I loved him. I loved him very dearly. And he died in Spain."

"Don't you have some photos of him? And weren't there some letters?"

"Your brother has them. Ask him." He hangs up.

When I receive a package of Dave's things from my brother, I'm excited, even though I don't know what I'm looking for or why. I sit down on my bed and undo the wrapping. The package includes letters, photographs, an announcement of Lillian Hellman's play *The Children's Hour*, a newspaper fragment about minstrel shows with comments by

Paul Robeson, and a harmonica. There are also flyers about a memorial meeting held in Dave's honor after his death, and the tiny pin I saw
years ago, with a Liberty Bell on it. I now see that across the top of the
pin are the words, "Friend—Abraham Lincoln Brigade."

I start reading the letters. My father translated them into English,
speaking aloud as my brother wrote it all down. The first one is to
my grandparents and is dated July 10, 1938. It begins:

> My dear Parents, I am sitting on a mountain among vineyards
> and olive trees covered with the blood of Spain. I am looking at
> the sunset and I weep, and weep and weep. I am crying with
> hot tears that are pouring out of my eyes and I don't want to
> stop that flow of tears, because I think of you, my dear parents.
> The thought of the pain and anguish I cause you and the
> thought that you think of me while you are reading this letter. I
> cry because I could not kiss you before I left because I could
> not tell you where I was going and not explain why I was
> going and I could not tell you what Spain means to you and to
> the whole world.

He ends the letter, "[F]orgive me, understand me and please don't be
angry."

How young he sounds. He regrets the kiss he couldn't give and no
doubt the one he didn't get, the blessing. He misses them. He's worried about their anger; he wants their forgiveness. How dear he must
have been. But it is his imagining them reading his letter that startles
me. Here is a psychologically astute boy with a talent for writing, as
well as a tender heart.

I begin to read another letter, dated two days later and addressed
to my father. "Dearest brother Lou!!!" it starts. I'm smiling. The
brothers. "It was indeed a great and unexpected joy to receive a letter
from you. Even though it has the taste of a trick to it. . . . In spite of

the fact that your letter was cold and brutally hard, unbrotherly and so business like, sharp and condemning. . . ."

I turn the letter over. This was to my father, who loved him more than anyone else in the world? There must be some mistake. My father wouldn't lie so completely, distort the very substance of his relationship with his brother. It isn't possible. I continue reading:

> I welcomed your letter heartily for I was deeply lonesome for you people, felt hurt and grieved because of the pain I caused Mom and Pop, and that cold farewell I got when I left New York—in spite of that coldness, I was overjoyed to hear from you. With my searching heart and eyes I did manage to find sparks of brotherly interest, concern, and ah—a bit of love. . . . Thanks—thanks a million. . . . Now perhaps when you are cooled off, you understand more and perhaps are sorry for accusing me of those things.

A bit of love? My father had written an unkind letter to him, a "cold and brutally hard" letter.

I call my father. "Dad, I have this odd letter in my hand from your brother . . ."

"Don't ask me about any letters!" he shouts. He slams the receiver down.

When I call again, he hisses into the phone, "I don't wish to unravel my intimate, cherished feelings to an individual like yourself."

3

DAVE IN THE ARCHIVE

I TELL MY friend Sharon, a photo curator at the New York Public Library, that I'm doing some work on the Abraham Lincoln Brigade, that I'm looking for information about my uncle, Dave Lipton. She beams, saying, "Well, aren't you lucky. We have the Randall Smith Archive here."

I look at her blankly.

"You know," she continues, "the Randall Smith Archive of the Abraham Lincoln Brigade?"

"Oh, yes," I lie, "I'll come tomorrow to take a look." In the afternoon that same day, Sharon comes hurrying over to me in the Wertheim Study, where I am working. "You're not going to believe this," she almost shouts, "we have a picture of your uncle. In a trench. You know how many people visit these archives searching for someone and never find anything? And there's your uncle, right there."

"How do you know it's him?"

She looks at me peculiarly and says, "His name is under the picture. What's the matter with you?"

"Well, thanks," I say, turning back to my book.

"Aren't you going to come look at it?"

DAVE IN THE ARCHIVE

I TELL MY friend Sharon, a photo curator at the New York Public Library, that I'm doing some work on the Abraham Lincoln Brigade, that I'm looking for information about my uncle, Dave Lipton. She beams, saying, "Well, aren't you lucky. We have the Randall Smith Archive here."

I look at her blankly.

"You know," she continues, "the Randall Smith Archive of the Abraham Lincoln Brigade?"

"Oh, yes," I lie, "I'll come tomorrow to take a look." In the afternoon that same day, Sharon comes hurrying over to me in the Wertheim Study, where I am working. "You're not going to believe this," she almost shouts, "we have a picture of your uncle. In a trench. You know how many people visit these archives searching for someone and never find anything? And there's your uncle, right there."

"How do you know it's him?"

She looks at me peculiarly and says, "His name is under the picture. What's the matter with you?"

"Well, thanks," I say, turning back to my book.

"Aren't you going to come look at it?"

33

"Now?" I ask.

"Yes, now," she says.

I don't want to get up. I wish Sharon would go away. But despite my shtetl ancestors pulling me back into the region of "Stay put. Don't make waves" and, yes, "He died for nothing," I do get up. I follow Sharon's long-legged, no-nonsense Norwegian stride—inherited from *her* ancestors—down the hall to the Art and Photography Room. There, in the rare books section where I have spent many a day poring over art books, Sharon has spread several oversized leather-bound albums of photographs of the Spanish Civil War across a long table. One volume is open, waiting for me.

"Here he is." Sharon points, beaming. "He looks like you."

I squint at a photograph of a man in profile, in a trench or leaning against the side of a hill. He's staring straight in front of him, over a low wall of banked earth, a gun at his shoulder. He wears a pointy cap. If "Dave Lipton" weren't scrawled beneath the photograph, there would be no way of knowing it's him. The sun has bleached away his features.

"Sharon, how can you say we resemble each other? You can't even see his face."

"Your bodies, the same proportions, the same ease, if you don't mind my saying so."

I look at the photo again. I see what she means. I like the grace and confidence of those lean limbs. There's no posturing, no tensed-up male strut, no tight clothes hugging bulging arms and torso. His physical nonchalance and neatness remind me of my father. If you didn't know he was a man, though, you might think him a slender girl. He stares in front of him, extra ammunition on his belt and at his feet next to a canteen. The weight of his body pushes against the earth and the brush of the hill. He's there to fight for the Spanish Republic. I don't know how he got here or why, but I don't mind considering it now, as cozy in this archive as I ever was as a girl alone in a movie palace in the Bronx. How very pleasant it is to

Abraham Lincoln Brigade Archive, Tamiment Library and Robert F. Wagner
Labor Archives, New York University

lounge in these roomy, curving wooden chairs, surrounded by waxed
library tables and the familiar smells of old books, near concerned
librarians whom I have known for thirty years.

I browse the albums, intrigued by old photos safely tucked into the
past, like the pictures we found as children in Hurleyville, pictures of
faraway places and elusive narratives. I turn the pages slowly, examining
photographs of men in combat, in camps and nearby towns, chatting
with villagers. I wonder who these people are, what are they doing
there in that mean, unloving landscape that calls the shots.

Near where the photograph of Dave has been taken, there are
others of men surveying the terrain, consulting one another in small
groups, aiming rifles. The lens captures some who are turned inward.
In one, a young man sits in sweat-soaked clothing, his head turning
toward a man in riding pants whose chest is crisscrossed with holster

Abraham Lincoln Brigade Archive, Tamiment Library and Robert F. Wagner Labor Archives, New York University

straps. Behind him and to his left, two men study a map. In the next instant—in another photo—he has turned, his fist now at his mouth, maybe in his mouth.

Here were people who had gone far away from home. They lost themselves in something larger and stranger than the lives they had known. They followed orders, their days were mapped out for them, and their job was simple yet wildly ambitious: take Spain back from the Fascists. They came from everywhere, forty thousand of them, Italian and German refugees from their by-then-Fascist countries, people from Yugoslavia, Czechoslovakia, Hungary, Cuba, the United States, Canada. Volunteers poured in. Whites, American blacks, Asians, Jews.

Most people wouldn't have done what they did. I wouldn't have. I find Sharon and thank her for her help.

Abraham Lincoln Brigade Archive, Tamiment Library and Robert F. Wagner Labor Archives, New York University

At the end of the week, I decide to take the bus to Boston, where there is a more extensive archive about the Abraham Lincoln Brigade at Brandeis University. This collection is crammed into a corner of the Judaic Studies Department office. I introduce myself to Victor Berch, the librarian, and say that I'm doing a little research on my uncle who died in Spain, a member of the brigade. I give him some publicity about my last book and show him photographs of Dave. Then I gingerly lift up a tattered flyer for Dave's memorial in the Bronx, on January 18, 1939. I can see that Mr. Berch is not impressed. He points to the three speakers listed on the flyer, David McKelvy White, Yale Stuart, and Bill Wheeler. "Dead. Dead. Dead," he says, pronouncing the words with some derision, as if it were my fault. I don't inform him that I am a historian, and I don't expect people to be alive. He tells me that if I'm interested, there's a videotaped interview of Wheeler made in 1986, as well as indexes and photographs I can consult.

I resist the impulse to flee the glum walls and ugly institutional furniture—the New York Public Library on Fifth Avenue this isn't. Instead, I unpack my papers in front of a window. I settle in and go over indexes, page through files, peruse more photographs. I see women nursing the wounded, bending over operating tables, leaning against ambulances, smoking cigarettes. I see men building trenches and cooking, carrying wounded comrades off battlefields, hiding in brambles. There are pictures of men taking showers, looking for all the world like classical Greek sculptures of boys seen in profile and from behind, their hairless, graceful chests like gently curving violins. Young is what they are, sturdy and vulnerable at the same time. I search for Dave's face. I try to picture someone from my family there, but I cannot. I move on to the types of people in Ken Loach's film, men who traveled to Spain inspired by their politics, goodwill, and unspoken longings, which they didn't or couldn't discuss. They elude me, until a few faces snag my attention. But I'm just picture gazing. I didn't know Dave, I never went to Spain, I've never risked my life for anything. The very words "risk my life" embarrass me.

Why am I trying to penetrate a new archive, always a daunting task? Where do I expect to take these photos of my uncle, his comrades, this inhospitable terrain? So much has been written about the Spanish Civil War already. I suppose I'm hoping to breathe life into a name that would normally be left a statistic in a fight during which thousands of people died for a belief, leaving a legacy that for many is holy. Perhaps I will be able to give my uncle a personality, attitudes, a taste in clothes and literature. Then, if people are interested, they can know another boy who shipped off on his own to fight for ideas he didn't have the heart to walk away from.

I am intrigued, even envious, that Dave left home the way he did. People call such acts courageous. What is courage if not the outward manifestation of an insistent desire that displaces one's need for security? Dave gave up security, love, and comfort, perhaps fled them, and put himself in a place where a hunger to fly slipped neatly into his politics, delivering him to a country lit up with political passion.

Amid the many photographs and records at Brandeis, I find my uncle's name several times. I'm surprised he is mentioned at all. He was only in Spain for three months before he was killed. He wasn't a leader. It's true that I haven't done much research at this point, but I have no sense from his letters home that he had any special position in Spain. Yet he keeps coming up. It's probably just one of history's accidents, I think to myself. Certain names, events, pictures float to the top, while others sink to the bottom. Some are saved, others destroyed by accident or intention. The ones you find become significant. But they aren't necessarily. I tell myself this.

Discovering a picture of Dave or a reference to him at Brandeis, though, isn't like finding traces of him in his parents' attic bedroom, a fluke of history, some friends or acquaintances taking pictures, someone preserving them. But it's almost the same thing, arbitrary in both cases, and evidence in both cases too. Still, the Brandeis archive feels more important. It's part of a public institution used by scholars, journalists, filmmakers. They are people who will create history even more, alas, than the people who were in Spain "risking their lives." That's a sad but incontrovertible fact. After all, no one today who wasn't there will ever know what actually happened. And even those who were there would only know a small piece of the picture, which could be interrogated by others, reinterpreted, sidelined, celebrated, or erased. Plus, of course, they would have done their own editing over the years as they negotiated the hills and valleys of their lives.

What constitutes "important," anyway? Who has the right to chronicle the past, to possess it as knowledge? Amusingly, Freud posed that question, trying to convince an audience of the efficacy of psychoanalysis as a study of individual personality, as a true way to know and help someone. For a contrast, he used the example of an esteemed professor lecturing on Alexander the Great. Why believe the professor, Freud asked, "who no more took part in Alexander's campaigns than you did"? Let's rather believe our analysts and ourselves as we observe, over years and decades, our personalities unfolding through our behavior, our dreams, and our relationship to our analysts.

I've been fascinated over the past several decades by a dramatic reinterpretation of former "facts" about Christianity, which emerged in the freshly available translated and annotated Gnostic Gospels, the Gospel of Mary and the Gospel of Judas. One reads them and finds a different Jesus—a rabbi—a wise and demanding Mary Magdalene, a sacrificial Judas. They emerge as Jews on the margin of history, arguing among themselves and with the hierarchy of their temple, not as saints, devils, or gods. Christianity doesn't have to exist in the form it has today. If that's true, then any aspect of the past can be reconfigured and reunderstood.

Well, here are some facts, some raw material, about Dave. He went to Spain on May 18, 1938. He took the baggy cotton clothes the Spanish Republicans handed him, the cap, and the gun, and when the leather of his shoes wore out, he tied *alpargatas* (what we call espadrilles) to his feet. He was my family's son, a boy from a good home, a neat, dutiful boy, a fine boy. Yet he burrowed through the walls of his Lifshitz life and leapt free, pushing his body across the Pyrenees, singing the marching songs of the International Brigades. He probably killed people. A Jewish boy killing people, and plenty of them. Yes, Israelis kill people, and King David was a warrior, but in my post-Holocaust brain, Jews do not kill. It's against the law. I look out the window at the sunny Brandeis campus. I see kids and yarmulkes, and I don't understand my uncle.

I never questioned my father's theology: "Nothing is worth dying for. Mind your own business." I didn't notice it. It was just the landscape I grew up in. I studied paintings, mostly Christian paintings. I let the gold backgrounds and angel wings and sweet Madonnas smooth over the rough spots of life, open up vistas where I wandered in peace or where I could hide and write and even fantasize that there was an afterlife. And then all of a sudden, there was Dave, right in front of my eyes, insisting on something else entirely, an altogether different way of being. Most people who believe in doing the right thing are like me, not like him. They do what they can safely at home. Why didn't he?

When I was growing up in the forties and fifties, I didn't want to make trouble. I know there is something Jewish in that. Maybe Dave wasn't inhibited in that way. Or else he didn't experience being Jewish as a limitation, though I find that hard to believe. The American poet Jacqueline Osherow knows what I'm talking about. She meditates on Piero della Francesca's frescoes, *The Legend of the True Cross*, in the Church of San Francesco in Arezzo, Italy. She revels in "Hats twirling, armor flying, coils of hair // Unraveling into whirling manes and tails—." But on an Italian tape recording in the church, she hears words about the fresco that disturb her, something about an "*ebreo*," a Jew. In the English version of the tape, "ebreo" is translated as "Judas." Osherow says she

> Put in a lot of coins to catch each syllable
> . . . .
> All the while not looking at the rope, the well;
>
> Instead, I chose a saintly woman's dress,
> An angel's finger pointing to a dream, . . .

Wise to herself, farther on Osherow discusses another troubling painting:

> I do have a fondness for the truth
>
> But am willing to make, in this case, an exception,
> Which has been, more or less, my people's way.
> We've learned to be remarkable at self-deception.

My people's way. We are *remarkable at self-deception.* American Jews en masse recoiled in fear after the Holocaust. We dove into art with a passion, and, to our credit, we changed American painting and literature. It is not easy to write poems or make paintings, but it's usually less dangerous than being shot at. I'd rather study pictures and write books. But I envy Dave. I just wish he hadn't died.

I tie up the portfolios I've been looking through, replace folders in boxes, and return them to the librarian. I ask to see the video interview of Bill Wheeler. Maybe there will be something in it for me. Wheeler stood up for Dave at the memorial meeting. I drop the cassette into the TV and find Wheeler, a man whose photographs I've already seen in the archive. And now here he is on the screen, fifty years further on. He's good-looking in his midseventies, plainspoken and direct, trustworthy in that American way that Europeans observe about us. There's no trace of an ethnic accent. I watch the tape dutifully, taking a few notes, waiting for something to jump out at me, but all I see is Wheeler's modesty. I turn off the video somewhere in the middle, when he describes returning to the States and deciding to go back to his parents' farm to help them out.

The archive at Brandeis astonishes me. Of the 2,800 Americans who went to Spain, a third were killed, and everyone knows that they were primarily Communists and that Americans detest and fear anything suggesting Marxism. Yet here is this collection of letters, photographs, taped and filmed interviews, books in many languages, posters. These godforsaken people—reviled as traitors in America, blacklisted in the forties and fifties, often forced to live in the underground—have their own archive, which they have managed to get into this politically moderate "Jewish" university. What stubbornness, what passion! It takes the breath away.

Those in the Judaic Studies Department probably have no idea what they have in this archive. Some powerful people who admire the Abraham Lincoln Brigade must have told a bureaucrat or two at the university that a high proportion of Jewish immigrants were involved, that it was important that the university house their papers. What Brandeis doesn't know is that as Communists, these men and women were discouraged from expressing interest in their religion or ethnicity. They were not like the African Americans in the brigade, whose race consciousness was cultivated. Canute Frankson from Detroit, for example, wrote of the Spanish children that they "felt so warm about me. Knowing that their little hearts were free from the black poison of race hatred meant so much to me." And Mississippian Eluard Luchelle McDaniels said, "I saw in the invaders of Spain the same people I've been fighting all my life. . . . I've seen lynching and starvation, and I know my people's enemies." Communism taught Jews to deny their difference as Jews, yet it encouraged blacks to see themselves as blacks, a sort of reverse racism and anti-Semitism all rolled up into one.

I leave Brandeis impressed but also disheartened. The Bill Wheeler tape bothers me. Even though, as Victor Berch said, Wheeler is dead now, I begrudge him his aliveness in the tape, when Dave vanishes more each day. Still, when I return to New York, I decide to visit the office of the Veterans of the Abraham Lincoln Brigade (VALB) on East Eleventh Street. Having started out as the Friends of the Abraham Lincoln Brigade immediately after the Spanish Civil War, the Friends are now VALB, a cohort often simply referred to as "the Vets." They are headquartered close to Union Square, that location in lower Manhattan so rich in American radical history.

I've spoken to one of the men, Abe Smorodin, on the phone. I also heard about him in the Wheeler video. Smorodin had been among the swiftest and most courageous runners in Spain, dealing with transmission problems, carrying information from one part of the battlefield to another, gathering officers for meetings. When I meet him, I see that he is a small, compactly built, no-nonsense sort of man. Yes, a runner. He's eighty-one, with one eye nearly blind since birth and another the color of black onyx, which fixes you with unwavering attention. I remove my photos and flyers from my briefcase and, to show him how in the know I am, I point to the three names on the flyer and repeat Berch's hortatory: "Dead. Dead. Dead."

"No." Abe shakes his head. "Wheeler's not dead."

"He's not? Where is he?" I'm shouting.

"I'll get you the address and phone number." In a few minutes, he returns, saying, "Look, here's the information about Bill, but here are a couple of other names of guys who were in the same company." When I'm almost out the door, he adds, "And where the hell were you twenty years ago? There were a lot more of us around then, and we had better memories."

I begin to answer—I was doing a PhD, I was a student, a feminist art history professor, a Marxist art historian—but I change my mind.

Just because Wheeler spoke at Dave's memorial doesn't mean he knew him, I say to myself on my way home. He was probably just doing his duty, the job of attending memorial services divided up among Veterans. Still, there was that proximity, Wheeler's name on the flyer next to Dave's. It's why I watched the video at Brandeis in the first place, why I scrutinized his face, his hands, the way he moved in his chair, his voice, his silences. I wanted to know him, though I see now that I was reluctant to admit it. I write to Wheeler:

Dear Mr. Wheeler,

I am working on a book about my uncle Dave Lipton who died in Spain during the Spanish Civil War. He was a member of the Abraham Lincoln Brigade and was in the First Platoon, Company 3. He died on August 20, 1938, near Gandesa on the Sierra Pandols.

I am trying to locate—at this late date alas—people who may remember him, however slightly. I'm enclosing a picture of Dave with his comrades.

I hope it's all right if I call you in a week or so and see if you can help me.

I look forward to speaking to you soon.

Sincerely yours . . .

I send out letters and photographs of Dave to other men in Company 3. John Murra, an anthropology professor emeritus at Cornell, responds, "I have looked repeatedly at the photograph of your uncle, Dave Lipton, but alas he is not a real presence. The moment in the 58th battalion's history reflected in the photograph is one that should be familiar—I was wounded only a few days earlier and some of the men I recall clearly. Not your uncle . . . Sorry."

Norman Berkowitz, a retired court stenographer who lives in Delray Beach, Florida, writes:

> The only thing I can say about Dave is that I remember his name, and I remember very vividly the night of his demise. On the evening of August 19th our company was sent up to a dug-in position to take a post there. Early in the morning we were suddenly attacked by the fascists and were almost surrounded. Our Sergeant, Jerry Cooke, gave the order to retreat. Only nine of us got back to the rest of our battalion. We never heard from any of those who didn't get back. . . . I seem to recall that Bill Wheeler was in the company. You can check that.

Jack Shafran doesn't respond. When I meet him in Spain in early November 1996, he says, "I had nothing to tell you. I didn't know him." The men I am speaking and writing to are nearly all in their eighties. Some in their nineties. Almost to a one, they respond, some with poems, others with reminiscences, a few tearfully. None knew Dave.

A week after I write to Wheeler, he faxes me: "I do remember your uncle Dave Lipton and now thanks to you, he has a name that time and a flagging memory have erased." I panic as the fax machine spits out these pages. I want to push them back in, and at the same time, I'm praying that the words falling out will change everything, that somehow, at the end, my uncle will not be dead.

Here is the rest of what Wheeler tells me:

Dave's death more than any of the too many others I have wit-
nessed has haunted me to this day. Dave and I first met aboard
the ship that was carrying several new volunteers and seven of us
who had been sent home and were returning for the second
time. That would have been early spring 1938.

Dave and I were both assigned to the 3rd company of the
Lincoln Washington battalion. After a short period of training,
about the end of June or beginning of July 1938, we assembled
on the banks of the Ebro River in preparation to launch the
Ebro offensive.

We were at rest the evening before the crossing. Dave handed
me a letter written in Yiddish asking me to mail it to his brother
(as I recall) if anything should happen to him. I remember telling
him "You will make it O.K. Just keep your head and fanny down."

The next morning he asked for the letter back and tore it to
bits. That morning we crossed the Ebro and proceeded on a three
day march with no food or water to the first town, abandoned by
the fascists as we approached.

We found some food, cans of salty fish but were unable to
drink the water as the fascists had contaminated all wells.

Tired, parched, and hungry we moved on to Hill 666, a rocky
height, completely barren of any vegetation due to the repeated
bombardment; not enough soil to dig trenches, the parapets piled
up rock that added to the danger when struck by artillery shells.

Company Three occupied the right flank of the battalion's
position. One of our squads was short handed and requested a
replacement. Dave's sergeant sent him to reinforce the squad.
While with that squad Dave was sent with a detail to the bottom
of the hill for grenades, much needed in the event of an attack.

It was shortly after this that I was checking our position at the
front when Dave walked over towards me asking if he could
return to his regular squad. Just as I yelled to him to get down, he

was struck by a sniper's bullet sinking slowly to the ground in front of me.

In war one becomes inured to death but Dave's has haunted me ever since. He was young, he was brave. . . .

Even after I read the phrase "Dave's death" at the beginning of the fax, I long to slow down what comes next, to hold on to the clarity of a spring sky at sea with my uncle, a day filled with optimism and excitement, if also with guilt about leaving his family. He'd been on a ship before. He had sailed to America with his mother in 1927, a couple of years after his father and brothers. He didn't get sick that time, when he was a boy with his mother. Perhaps he wouldn't this time, either. Maybe his eye lingers on the wooden rails and planked floors of the ship, recalling his friend Ben Katine's skill with a saw and lathe. He might notice the ship's long, horizontal Chicago-style windows. Maybe the artfully arrayed artificial light inside entices him—romantic here, practical there—and the dramatic spaces, inviting furniture, all of it buffering the passengers against the vagaries of nature just outside. Men and women together, the heat and expectation of it. Flesh and glitter in plain view, plunging necklines and shapely ankles, pearl necklaces and gold cuff links. He's not supposed to admire such trappings of materialist pleasure, but maybe he does, some pull at his senses beyond his control. He knows that staring at the sea is dangerous for him, takes him places he'd rather not go. He is better at meeting people. He picks out the other men going over but is not obvious in his acknowledgment. They were told to be extremely careful. With each face he finds, he travels a little farther from home. And perhaps one day, meandering aimlessly on deck, he decides, uncharacteristically, to go to the bar.

"Hi. Mind if I join you?" Dave asks a man drinking a beer.

"Not at all. How're you doing?" The man almost adds *son*.

"Fine. Thank you."

"What's your name?"

"Dave, Dave Lipton. I'm from New York. Listen, I know we're not supposed to talk to each other, but . . ."

The man nods and says, "Sure. What are you drinking?"

"I'll have a Coke. You're Bill Wheeler, aren't you?"

"Yup, that's me. How did you know? There ain't no sign, is there?" He laughs shyly.

"No." Dave's gullible. "One of the others pointed you out. I know you were there before." (Bill was shot several times at the Battle of Jarama in February 1937.)

Dave wants to ask Wheeler questions. He wants to know what's coming up.

"It'll be harder this time than the last, you can be sure of that," says Wheeler, not looking into the boy's eyes. "Now that the French border is closed. Last time it was a marvelous thing crossing over into Spain, people waving, giving you the Popular Front salute, the raised fist. Everyone turned out to see us go, to cheer us on. Even the mayor. This time, though, what with the French declaring neutrality, I don't know. As far as when you get to Spain, I'm sure you'll have a training period, probably relatively short. Do you know how to fire a gun?"

"Yes I do."

My uncle is modest, soft-spoken. Wheeler's seen other Americans like him in Spain. Many. Theirs is not a macho outfit.

"What language besides Spanish are people speaking over there?" Dave asks.

"English, French, and Yiddish. That's what I heard."

Dave smiles. "Really? Well, I guess I'm safe there. I can manage in German and Spanish too."

"Well, I'd say you're pretty prepared. More than most."

"I wish we were there already."

"Ever see a man die?" Wheeler asks.

Dave looks down. "No, but I'm not afraid. I know that about

myself. I don't know why I say that, but I know I'll be a good soldier."

"I'm sure you will." Wheeler reaches across and pats Dave on the shoulder.

"Well, nice to talk with you. I won't keep you anymore," Dave says. He gets up.

"Any time." Wheeler again stops himself from saying *son*.

Dave arrives in Spain and exerts his body on the hot foreign soil, a gun in his hand, strange languages at his ears. Writing in Yiddish to my father, carefully crafting the words, saying something important, meaning it for his eyes, for his heart. Giving it to a new friend, a trusted comrade. Nervously, anxiously, embarrassedly retrieving it, tearing it to pieces, "to bits." Hot and thirsty, descending a dry, naked hill with other men, trusted, carrying grenades. Trusted. Then, the sniper. Slowly, inexorably, sinking.

Wheeler's considered words spread across the page, side by side in front of me, this remnant of my uncle given to me. I meet the man who stood near him, perhaps heard him at the end, touched him. Was there a moan, a cry? Will Wheeler ever describe to me the consternation on the boy's face or the horror, the knowledge, and the sorrow of losing . . . everything? Wheeler watching his face go from life to nothing, tumbling downward . . . downward.

There's a witness. I want to call my father and tell him I've found Bill Wheeler. I found Dave's friend, Dad. He had a friend before he died. He wasn't alone. And he was brave. Wheeler says so. But what about that letter? Why did he tear it up? What was he doing? Saying something he was uncertain about? Something angry? Were they just words of love and good-bye that he thought might undermine his resolve, bring him bad luck? Or was this a letter like that first one my father sent him, the one that was "brutally hard, unbrotherly"?

I call my father. I talk about Wheeler. My father is silent.

"Why do you care about all this?" he asks quietly.

"I don't know, Dad. It's interesting."

Why do I care? Because my uncle was brave? Because his decision enthralls me, the journey intrigues me, the optimism amazes me? I don't know. Do I suspect that there is another narrative, even more enticing than the story I've been given? And that this hidden tale is discoverable, that I can uncover it, dust it off, stand it up, and march it into plain view?

Wheeler writes that he's haunted by the boy and has been all his life. If he saw so many die, why has Dave lingered with him? What was unusual about him? I order a copy of the video from Brandeis, and this time I watch it to the end. Wheeler talks about coming home, the awful sadness of it, knowing they had lost. He remembers meeting a pal from Spain at a demonstration at Union Square. The friend was going to California to help organize the grape growers, and Wheeler decided to go too. He talks about meeting his second wife, Ione.

The last question the interviewer asks is "What stays with you the most from your experience in Spain, Bill?" And Wheeler says this: "I was out checking some of the positions, and this boy came walking over slow and measured and he said, Bill, can I go back to my squad? He was standing there. And just as I was about to yell at him to get down, a sniper got him. He stood there yelling, *No, no, no*, and fell right there at my feet."

The tape goes grainy. I pick up the phone to call Bill Wheeler in Athens, Georgia. It has been a week since I received the fax.

I introduce myself. We are polite. We fall silent.

"Bill," I call him, "I can't believe I've found you. After all these years."

"It's odd, isn't it?" he says.

"Bill, I . . ." I'm crying. I can hear that he is too. We sit in our separate worlds, lonely for our pasts, which are so tenuously connected yet somehow kindred. We both lived the death of my uncle but also the glory of a past long gone for one, never experienced by the other, yet cherished.

"Bill, I'd like to come talk with you."

"Please."

Bill lives with Ione and their daughter, Lauren. They moved to Athens a year and a half earlier from Southern California, where they had spent their lives. Bill had been a union organizer and worker for a Ford tractor company, Ione a social worker. When we meet, they are both eighty-six. He is erect and agile, bending down to a low shelf and getting up again with ease that a man of fifty would envy. His hair is close cropped. He's trim. We sit in a living room that has several comfortable chairs, two sofas on either side of the TV, a few carefully hung photographs, and a couple of modest paintings. We place ourselves close together near a large window facing out to the front of the house. It's summer, Georgia, and the world is still. We're alone in the room, hardly knowing each other, waiting to talk.

Bill tells me that he left the party at the end of the 1950s, after Khrushchev disclosed the atrocities of Stalin's regime. But he remained committed to leftist causes. With other Veterans of the Abraham Lincoln Brigade, he raised money to send ambulances to Nicaragua, and in 1988, he delivered the last eight of them with some friends. He demonstrated against the first Gulf War. He supports an end to the embargo on Cuba, which seventeen years after his death in 1998 actually begins to happen. Although he is not a naturally verbal person, he goes to neighborhood schools when invited, talks about Spain, about the willing men and women who traveled far to fight Fascism. Recently he spoke at the local Unitarian church. He's not sentimental, but he remembers, and he wants America to know about the brigade. He's a small part of the machinery that has landed the Vets' archives in places like Brandeis, the New York Public Library, and now NYU.

Despite the brigade's long-standing identification with the Communist Party, their continuing commitment to progressive political work and the optimism and respectfulness of people like Bill have gone far to persuade schools, churches, publishers, and archives to value what the brigade did and recognize what an important piece of American history it represents. They were brave and honorable people. Americans should know about this part of American history.

"Bill, do you recall how Dave struck you when you first met him?" I ask.

"No. I just know that we met on the ship, and he questioned me about what he might expect over there. He may have found me because I was returning a second time, and I had been an officer. I don't know how we met. We weren't supposed to associate closely on board, we were supposed to be tourists, that's all. We hung out some, but we were circumspect. I was traveling with a false passport."

"Did he seem to be an anxious person?" I'm curious if people trusted my uncle when they met him. Did they see in his face something they could go by, read word for word? Did they get what they expected? Or did he look away when he thought someone turned toward him? Was there something under his arm, inside his coat that he was hiding, holding back?

"No. He was rather quiet and introspective, it seemed to me. What little I knew him. He was sort of measuring himself. That's as far as I can go." Bill won't embellish—the crew cut, the directness, the uncluttered precision. In quick succession, I hear that they landed in Le Havre, spent a day and night in Paris on the Right Bank, and were brought through France toward Spain by French Communists.

"We were taken to the south, but not as far as Perpignan," he says, where he had gone on his first trip over. "In the foothills of the Pyrenees, we went to this big old French farmhouse, and the farmer's young daughter fed us. While we were in the barn waiting for dark, there was a knock at the door, and the girl came in and said, 'Shh, the

Fascists.' After a while, when it was dark, she slipped in again and whispered, '*Allez, allez.*' . . ." Go.

I'm not listening. I'm stuck on the fact that Dave had been in Paris—in the city where I now live, the city my father couldn't stop talking about when I was growing up. What might Paris have meant to Dave? He was on his way to Spain, to spring forward into another life, this youngest son of a large family. Finally, a chance to make a difference, to help, maybe to stand out, to be more like Phil the doctor, Louis the charmer. Maybe Paris was an irritation, a resented detour.

People did call Riga, his birthplace, the Paris of the North. And Paris was the city of myth and revolution so valued by the Left, specifically the revolutions of 1789, 1830, 1848, as well as the Commune of 1871. Marx wrote his *Eighteenth Brumaire* when the Revolution of 1848 failed in France. The Commune became a model of a proletarian uprising for him.

Paris was the capital of a country that had passed extraordinary social legislation in the 1930s—paid summer vacations, a 12 percent pay raise, nationalization of the Bank of France, a forty-hour work week. I moved to Paris because of its remarkable political history, and for the pleasures of daily life.

The French past meant a lot to the members of the Lincoln Brigade. Robert Colodny, a Vet who became a history professor, wrote, "From the beginning the physical as well as spiritual headquarters of the volunteers was Paris." That was where "the illegal political parties of eastern and central Europe had their centers of political organization, their press, and their greatest concentrations of émigrés . . . [where] the first volunteers were provided with the credentials and directions for the journey to Barcelona."

And Paris is the city of love. Dave was a young man.

"Bill, could we return to Paris for a minute? What did you do there? Paris is a city my family reveres. I would love to be able to place Dave there. Isn't there anything you can recall? The neighborhood you stayed in, a restaurant or café, what the weather was like?"

Bill looks away, his desire to end the conversation palpable. Instead, he turns toward me and says, "There was something interesting when we got to Paris. We went for a walk together around town, and he seemed to be quite concerned that . . . here he was, twenty-two years old and going to war and . . . he'd never slept with a woman. I, uh, helped him find a poor little streetwalker who turned out to be a very sad young woman, and I don't think it was a very rewarding experience. I have that feeling. He was concerned about it, going to war, and that he hadn't lived that much. I was about four years older than him."

"He told you that? You'd think he'd have been embarrassed."

"Well, we felt comfortable with each other. We liked one another."

My uncle, twenty-two and a virgin. And with a brother like my father. I wonder why it is so hard to drag this information from Bill. Perhaps it is just his modesty, or his desire to protect the privacy of his dead friend, who might have been embarrassed to have people know this detail of his life. But maybe there is more, something I am not getting. It is difficult to fill in the blanks in Bill's spare account. We are people from distinct worlds. Different things touch us, demand our responses.

Still, Dave, there in Paris. A stretch of time between New York and Spain, between his family and . . . what? Some sort of hope, some fulfillment that was distinct from his political work in New York, something that was all his own. There was, it seems, some hankering in my uncle to matter, to fly away. To live.

4

BRONX CALLS

WHEN I WAS a little girl and living with my grandparents in Hurley-ville, my grandma and I would often sit outside in early winter, taking the sun. I remember her wearing her old mouton coat and crocheting, the sunlight glinting off her wire-rimmed glasses.

I wear my snowsuit and sit at the back of an old metal chair, my feet sticking out. One day, burbling away, I ask Grandma why she has no friends.

"Mommy has friends," I say, squinting up at her.

"I don't need friends," she says, "and neither does your mommy."

I wriggle around in my seat, turning toward the snow-heavy fir tree. I watch a bird burst out of the tree's floppy branches and dart over to the maple on the other side. The bird, scanning the tree for a spot to rest, is probably as surprised as I am at the balancing act exe-cuted by the load of new snow. Icicles hang from the red tin roof of our house, and our large orange cat, Pincey—all our cats have this name, as one by one, each is routinely killed by a car or a wood-chuck—suns herself on the porch railing.

Grandma usually keeps to herself, absorbed in personal and domestic activities. In a corner of our warm kitchen, she rides the pedal on her Singer sewing machine, twisting and turning fabric like a real tailor. She kneads her bread dough confidently, she brushes my hair with love and her own with a passion. She rarely smiles. But like my father, she has an amused twinkle in her eyes. She can have fun with someone.

When I think of my mother, I picture her far away in the city, sitting at the kitchen table in the Bronx, smoking. She picks a trace of cigarette paper off her lower lip, sips coffee, and stares out the window at the brick wall of the neighboring building. She waits for my father. But she certainly does have friends. Her closest ones are Betty and Doris. Tiny Betty, a rabble-rousing Communist out on the streets but struck dumb at meetings and in the face of her husband's meanness. Trim Doris, ever marrying up, moving from the Bronx to Chicago and endlessly giving my mother, Trudy, sober, unasked-for advice over the phone, which my mom never takes.

Dave had been my mother's friend. Did my grandma know that?

Having found friends all her life, on her dying day, my ninety-year-old mother initiated what she hoped would be a new friendship with her African American nurse, and in her unsteady, still-husky voice, she shared her considered opinions about race in America. She was the only white person I knew who had African American friends.

Louis, they say, like his mother, needed no one. "He was tough and suspicious," a cousin reports. "He judged things always in terms of himself. 'What's in it for me?' he'd ask first of all." This same cousin describes Grandma as *farbissine*—scheming and distrustful—someone who believed only in hard work. Few people had sympathy for her. My father and grandma had the habits of skeptical immigrants. So did Phil, another disagreeable Lifshitz.

Dave, on the other hand, trusted people. "He was a happy guy brimming with boyish charm," another cousin says. "He was more sincere than Louis." My mother loved Dave unreservedly. "What a nice man he was," she said. The more I hear about him from my family, the less I feel I know him. It's all so predictable and even a bit thin. Where are the knots and contradictions that would fuel the decisions Dave made? Where is any hint of darkness and uncertainty? And egotism? Maybe my mother had it right when she said, sighing, "After he died, the family closed the book."

Nonetheless, finding Bill inspires me to keep going.

I examine a list of people who made donations for Spanish refugees in Dave's memory soon after the war was over. I note names on letters and envelopes and newspaper clippings that were in the shoebox. If his friends and acquaintances are still around, they are between seventy-five and ninety. I start with New York City telephone books. It's 1994. Later, I'll use the Internet. I find an unexpected number of people, long-lived men and women who became editors, teachers, union organizers, builders, social workers, childcare professionals, foundation officers. They are retired now, but many have stayed in New York, bound by their history in the city and its radicalism. Others live in and around Miami, in Southern California, in upstate New York and New York City. Sometimes I meet these people face to face. More often, we write to each other, speak on the phone, exchange e-mails. To a person, they want to talk about my uncle.

Particularly helpful initially is a man I happen on by accident at *Jewish Currents*, a small progressive magazine that has been in publication since 1946. Its editor, Morris Schappes, was a teacher at City College when my uncle was said to have gone there. It is by mere chance that I encounter Eddy Meskin on the phone one day when I am looking for Schappes, his ninety-three-year-old boss. When Meskin answers and I say who I am and that I'm Dave Lipton's niece, I can practically hear him smiling before he says, "I knew your uncle Dave. He was a great guy. He had a great head of blond hair, too!"

Meskin's voice is eager and nervous. He is eighty-one years old. We make a date to meet. As we are about to hang up, he mentions a woman who knew Dave. "Evelyn. That's what she was called," he remembers. He's not sure of her last name, but he gives me the number of someone who might help me out.

I have already learned that Dave was an active member of the YCL, the Young Communist League. When I meet Eddy in person for coffee, he tells me, "Dave was one of the leaders in our club, always busy, always with some party literature in his back pocket. You know," he adds, smiling, "our clubs were originally called 'branches,' but by the mid-1930s, we were trying to be more American, more fun, so we decided to call ourselves a club."

Herman Chermak, one of the younger members of the YCL in Dave's time, says, "A person was a 'nothing' in those days if they weren't involved in politics." Chermak's mother and Dave's knew each other from the IWO, the International Workers Order, a social and cultural group like the socialist Workmen's Circle, only Communist. One person describes a picket line at a local butcher shop that Dave helped organize. Someone else remembers him assisting people who had been thrown out of their apartments for not paying rent for several months. YCLers worked hard to stop evictions and to organize tenants.

"If a family was evicted," Quincy Goldberg, a friend of Dave's who now lives in Miami, says, "we would take them to the Home Relief Bureau and make sure they got what they deserved. We studied the rules and were insistent that they be followed. For example, that they had a right to get money for rent and find emergency shelter, and so on." If these young activists passed a sidewalk where furniture was piled high and the police were nowhere in sight, they would carry the furniture back into the apartment. The landlord then had to wait six months to start eviction procedures again. This created an unpredictable situation; there was always the possibility of jail.

Goldberg, who had been born in 1914 in New York to Lithuanian and Russian parents, was also active with Dave in the unemployed movement. The Communist-coordinated unemployed councils organized street demonstrations and led classes for people who had lost their jobs. Their goal was to show middle-class America who the unemployed were and that they existed in large numbers and desperate conditions. They also meant to build workers' confidence and suggest, along the way, that the problems they faced were not their fault but were peculiar to the capitalist system. Blame the bosses, not yourself, they urged. The councils proposed the idea that the government should provide a safety net for people who lose their jobs, and workers should be paid if prevented from working. Fraser Ottanelli, a historian, writes, "In some cities local councils were so strong that landlords would try unsuccessfully to secure their permission before evicting tenants."

One can hardly appreciate now the uniqueness of tenant-relief organizations and worker councils in the early 1930s. It might be easier to comprehend their novelty if we try to imagine an organization today whose stated goal is to help people who are losing their homes because they were duped by mortgage scalpers and their sophisticated partners on Wall Street. The relief organizations and councils influenced FDR's New Deal legislation in the midthirties, programs like the Social Security system, the Federal Deposit Insurance Corporation, the Federal Housing Administration, and the Securities and Exchange Commission. Many say that Roosevelt was able to institute his programs because it was thought that they might prevent the country from going even farther to the left.

Dave and Quincy worked at the councils handling grievances and educating tenants about their rights. Both had also worked as waiters in the Catskills, in the summers of 1936 and 1937. Quincy describes Dave as "articulate" and a "devoted guy," a man who "wasn't naïve in the slightest. He knew what he was doing. He didn't speak publicly, though. It wasn't his thing." Quincy often repeats that "Dave was good-natured, someone who laughed a lot." But he also noticed that

Dave was growing increasingly frustrated that he wasn't finding a paying job and impatient with the endless talk, talk, talk among the comrades, especially as things grew worse in Europe.

Quincy's measured phrases come up through the telephone wires to me: "Yeah, we hung around a lot. We talked politics endlessly. It was a small, narrow group and we weren't romantically inclined. It was what you might call masculine bonding, mostly."

Louis and Phil also noticed that Dave felt uncomfortable living off the family and not having salaried work. He worked a little for my mother's father at his fruit stand but didn't like it. Something about my grandfather and the Mafia. He also did some clerical work for the Warehouse and Wholesale Employees Union. Rose Morrison, a secretary there, remembers Dave as "a gentle, serious person, quiet, friendly, with a quick smile. He laughed at my jokes, and I really appreciated that."

In 1935, Dave's mother wrote to one of her brothers in Riga, asking him about the possibility of Dave studying airplane mechanics in the Soviet Union. I learned of the existence of this letter from the response Dave received from Grandma's nephew, seventeen-year-old Yasha: "[Your mother] says that you want to study mechanics [in general] and airplane mechanics and that you want to travel to Russia. If you can work this out, this would be the best thing in the world . . . it is the best trade. Don't listen to what my father writes you, that you should study car mechanics . . . he's afraid to fly in an airplane."

Certainly, it would have been easier for Dave's parents to accept his moving to Russia than his volunteering for a war that his American passport, stamped "Not for Travel in Spain," forbade him from participating in. Dave might have been irritated with himself for not pursuing the Russian possibility more.

Quincy remembers one evening after a meeting when Dave and some friends are at the Red Bagel on Southern Boulevard and Tremont Avenue in the Bronx, a favorite hangout. They start discussing

Hitler and Mussolini and what's happening in Spain. Quincy asks Dave if he's still thinking of going to Russia, something he mentioned a few weeks earlier.

Dave replies, "No, I heard from my uncle Dovid who lives there. He told me to continue doing what I'm doing here. He doesn't realize how little we do, how much we just sit around and talk, at meetings, here, on street corners. Face it, that's what we do."

"Maybe." Quincy smiles. He can't deny it, but to Dave, he says, "We learn while we talk, don't we? Plus, come on, we do good work. With the unemployed and the evicted. We do something. And you don't think educating young people about Fascism is important?" He's pushing it here. He knows most kids don't care.

"Maybe. I dunno," Dave says. "I wish I could get some experience building airplanes."

"Airplanes? Where'd you get that from?" chimes in Mike Silver, the youngest among them at sixteen. He's only been out of the Bronx to go to Manhattan a couple of times.

"Well, I'm a mechanic, you know."

"Go on!" says Mike. "You got an academic diploma, just like I'm working on."

"I do, but I went to the de Hirsch School afterward to learn mechanics," says Dave.

"Really?" Quincy asks. He realizes that there's a lot he doesn't know about Dave.

I ask acquaintances to be specific about Dave's demeanor. They look perplexed. They don't remember, they say. It's not the sort of observation that interests them. Like Bill Wheeler. No one can describe what Dave was like coming into a room or the timbre of his voice, anything about his diction or specifics about how he defended his opinions. What they remember is gentleness and commitment, a certain mildness of manner. When I reach Dave's friend

Evelyn Schein by phone—the woman whose last name had eluded Eddy Meskin—and announce to her that I'm doing research on Dave Lipton, she gasps, "Dave's been on my mind all these years. I can't believe you've found me. You've made my life worthwhile." Then she confides, "I never knew a man like him, so soft and kind and good." Those are exactly my mother's feelings.

Evelyn is seventy-five when I meet her, a large woman who chooses her words carefully. She is the only person among those I interview who insists that I not use her real name. Her modest home near Boston is located in what used to be a left-wing community. Before retiring, she worked in early-childhood education and ultimately became the director of a daycare center. She met Dave in 1937 at the leadership training school of the YCL. She was fifteen, he twenty-two.

Evelyn and I sit together on her screened-in porch in midsummer. She places some fruit on a plate. Littering the oil cloth–covered table are newspapers, planters, bills, and books. I'm struck by how willing she is to talk, especially considering her anxiety about concealing her identity. Every former comrade of Dave's whom I meet is eager to talk. The Cold War and McCarthy made them cautious, but Spain still means an immense amount to them, and they're not afraid to talk about it. It's obvious that they hope that someday, it will be important to other Americans. Fighting what came to be referred to as the Good Fight does have an American ring to it. Americans believe that's the kind of struggle they're up for. They did fight in World Wars I and II. Surely one day, they will want to know about the role of their compatriots in the Spanish Civil War, when a few thousand of their countrymen and -women volunteered, traveling at their own expense to Spain to defend what were, after all, American values: "Life, Liberty, and the Pursuit of Happiness." And the Veterans, those left-wingers and liberals who went to Spain, had been right. If only the French, English, and Americans had done something to stop Franco, Fascism might not have thrived, and Hitler's ferocious ambitions might have been crushed.

"I'd be early for a class and hiding behind a book," Evelyn tells me. "I had things to say when necessary, but I was shy. Dave would come over and talk to me. It meant a lot. And it wasn't easy in those situations. The men were always vying for the limelight. But not him. He wasn't a flashy, talky, leaderly type. He was dependable, constant. He never raised his voice. He listened. . . . The others could be ruthless."

I'm reminded of a discussion that one of Dave's friends mentioned to me. It had taken place at the Red Bagel. It started with male chauvinism and wound up, as often happened, with Spain.

Mike says, "That was some debate at the last meeting, wasn't it?"

"It won't go anywhere," says Quincy, tapping the table.

"It should, it's important," Dave responds, hugging a pile of *Daily Workers* he's been selling.

"You really think so?" Another guy's ears prick up. "I mean, it's important to respect the girls, but why make a big deal about it, especially concerning someone like Bob, who's such a great guy?"

"What, he's beyond criticism?" Dave bristles, putting the papers down. "He should show more respect. Girls like to be taken seriously, and they should be."

"Yeah, sure," Quincy says.

"What do you think about Spain?" Herman asks. He's the guy whose mother knows my grandma through the International Workers Order. Dave looks over at him.

"It's a damn shame," he says, shaking his head. "I don't know why more of us don't go."

"Our parents would kill us, that's why," Mike chimes in.

"Well, not you," says Dave, "you're too young. But others of us. It would be the right thing." His voice has gone thick and husky. Everyone at the table is staring at him now.

"I am thinking about it," he admits.

"With your mother? She'll pinch you black and blue," Herman says. They all laugh. They know Mrs. Lifshitz to be a fierce woman, herself a Communist sympathizer, but Dave feels instinctively—as the others do—that she won't let him go. She'll find reasons. His mother wants what all mothers want for their sons: a steady job, marriage, children.

I ask Evelyn if she was sexually drawn to Dave. No, she says, it was never like that. I don't ask why. There are men with whom women feel comfortable, and those women are grateful. Dave seems to have been such a man, and Evelyn strikes me as a woman who would have appreciated him, a woman who was inhibited by the authority of men yet attracted to authoritative men at the same time.

"Call Bob Schrank," Evelyn suggests with a half-disgusted, half-teasing look. This, it turns out, is the "Bob" who had been at the center of the male-chauvinism discussion at the Red Bagel.

I track Bob Schrank down and call. A blustery man whom I know to be in his eighties barks at me across the line. He had been a leader in the YCL when Dave was a member. He abandoned his left-wing politics long ago and is sarcastic about everything, yet as soon as I mention Dave's name, his gruffness evaporates. "Dave was gentle and sweet, an innocent," he says. "His humanity always came out. You felt it all the time. Anyone who knew him loved him. He was our angel, our sweet, loving David."

Dave wrote to Bob from Spain. Dave also sent him the photograph with Ben Katine that I had seen as a child, the one where Dave is so thin and fragile looking. It was made into a postcard, and on the back, Dave wrote, "July 4, 1938, 5pm. To my Comrade Bob Schrank—both of us are enveloped in our common fight against fascism!! Dave Lipton." The stilted language is different from what I've encountered in Dave's letter writing and the tone invoked by friends' descriptions of him. He seems to be bragging here to someone he admires, and he's doing an awkward job of it. Nevertheless, it was the Fourth of July. Perhaps Dave was making an American gesture with his postcard.

Dave, "an angel." In my family. That's hard to believe. Both the benevolence and the apparent sexlessness. It's true that my grandfather

was a humane, easygoing man. People felt safe with him. He was amiable and old-fashioned, in his vest, with his smooth, round watch on a gold chain tucked into a pocket and absent-mindedly stroked from time to time. He moved slowly, every tilt of his head, every gesture of his hands, self-contained. People trusted him. When he came into my father's luncheonette and the two hugged, Grandpa put his hand on my father's back as if he were a little boy, and my father's body would go calm for a miraculous moment. He was a man to give a woman confidence and let her be, much as Evelyn described Dave. But there was also an indifference in my grandfather, an opacity and self-absorption. He floated above the Lifshitz melee like the old Jew drifting across the skies of Marc Chagall's Russian shtetl. My sense is that he was more present than Dave, less hesitant in his body and appetites, at least apropos the Dave we hear about, before he went to Spain. My grandpa could also get extremely irritated sometimes, and occasionally surprisingly nasty.

No one would ever describe my father as an angel. Dave and Lou didn't have much in common, except for their physiques. Louis pushed into things without reflection; Dave held back, watched, and waited. Louis expected the worst from people, Dave the best. Dad was acerbic and witty, Dave plainspoken and earnest. Perhaps there were moments when my father relaxed, breathed more easily in the presence of his younger brother. He might have marveled at him the way he did at Alyosha in Dostoyevsky's *Brothers Karamazov*, the benevolence and diffidence, the absence of vanity, the generosity of spirit. But my father demanded something harder of himself, although it comprised the thinnest of covers and was always on the verge of disintegrating. I knew my father had a more romantic side, that he was also the man who kept a special piece of soap in a drawer, which he would take out and smell from time to time, reminding him of something or someone. And when we read great literature together, another man slipped out, the one who wanted to be a thinker, a poet, a hero. He longed to be a writer. He was drawn to my first husband, whose lithe body and mild manner perhaps reminded him of Dave and whose writerly ambitions nudged his own. It wasn't the Louis most people knew, nor was it the Louis he wanted the world to know. But it was real enough.

I also knew that my father was a fearful person. He turned up in a dream of mine trying to crawl out of a high window, just as I cried to him for help. *That's* not my father, I thought. But then I realized, yes, it is. Such a man might have been deeply in awe of a brother who decided to fight in the Spanish Civil War, maybe envious too. And angry. Dave probably had no idea.

Bob, who calls Dave an angel, also says, "Dave wasn't an adventurer. He was a contemplative person. He evoked in you a feeling of 'What can we do for you? Come on, Dave, what can we do for you?'" Bob was younger than Dave by a year or two. He was one of the few working-class members in the YCL, and he was the Bronx-wide leader for education. Perhaps his confidence and swagger brought out the younger brother in Dave. Maybe Bob reminded him of Lou.

I learn from Bob that Dave sought him out for advice about Spain. "After one of my speeches, Dave came into Hymie's, a delicatessen we'd go to on Tremont near Prospect," Bob says. "He wanted to speak to me about something. I was with a bunch of people, but I said, 'Okay,' and forgot about him. He waited and waited. It got to be 1 a.m. Now, it turns out, I was having a little affair with a YCL girl, so I wasn't particularly interested in talking to Dave. I was interested in walking her home and stopping in the park for a while. When the girl and me left, Dave walked along with us and said he wanted to talk to me. 'What's so important?' I asked. He said he had to decide whether to go to Spain or not. I said, 'Why are you asking me?'" Dave looked at him, bewildered. "'Because you speak so powerfully against Fascism.'" Bob announced that he was a pacifist and couldn't tell Dave what to do.

Nonetheless, Dave wrote Bob from Spain. It was a two-part letter. The beginning was addressed specifically to him, but the longer, more detailed and evocative section was to his YCL group of intimates in general. At the end of the first part, Dave wrote, "Be sure to show this letter with my regards and apologies to Al Steele, Lou Malinow, Ethyl Katon, Willie, Rosalie, Norman, [Evelyn Schein] . . . and ask them please to drop me a letter and I'll be sure to answer them." (The underlining is in the original.)

Dave described in great and colorful detail what he saw in Spain and then, more earnestly, what he was learning. "Here I have learned the true meaning of International Solidarity," he wrote.

How great and powerful proletarian discipline can be you cannot imagine unless you experience it. . . . We have daily political hours, practice in the field, practice on the blackboard. All unnecessary discipline and compulsory hardships are gone. You walk, talk, and live as a human being and that makes you a damn good soldier. . . . Political training is very important here. We have political commissars [and] cultural leaders . . . we are encouraged to read and study and live as comrades. . . . We are here not only as soldiers of war but soldiers of explanation, sacrifice, understanding, proletarian discipline, unselfishness, pep, and comradeship.

Then he makes a shy request: "If we have anything, we share and I too would like to give my part. Most comrades expect parcels from the U.S. I would also appreciate it if you comrades would send me articles such as any food stuff that can keep, chocolate, cigarettes, tobacco, etc. . . ."

Evelyn only sees the letter to Bob sixty years later, when I send it to her. "Dave was committed," she says. "We all were then. It was our life. It gave us a reason to be alive. To help people, to make a difference. We were proud of ourselves, and hopeful. But the truth is, I was surprised when I heard he left. People often said at the time, in 1938, that those who went to Spain then went to die. That they knew they would die. The Republicans had already lost."

Dave hadn't told Evelyn he was leaving. She felt left out and hurt when she learned that he'd gone. Now she realizes that he remembered her. She also sees that she could have helped him, written to him, sent him cigarettes, chocolate, clothing. Why hadn't Bob shared the letter? Her face tenses into an involuntary grimace. Then she weeps. Even now, people want to remember Spain and who they and their friends were then.

Quincy also regrets not seeing that letter. "Dave was a little older than the others. He was very committed." He looks down at his hands. "He was one of the few who went from the neighborhood. He felt guilty that he wasn't doing enough. He wanted to take his place on the front lines. You know, the final place to show your dedication was Spain. I think he was disappointed in me that I didn't go." It's as if it were yesterday.

In Spain, Dave expressed his strong feelings toward his comrades in New York. At the end of his letter to them, he wrote, "I am the interpreter here when German is spoken . . . my knowledge of both [Spanish and German] comes in handy . . . I made a temporary corporal—thus am I representing the Bronx YCL in Spain!!!!"

In his memoir, Bob writes, "At YCL headquarters I heard that Dave Lipton was killed after a few weeks. . . . I have no idea how long I sat in the toilet and cried for Dave." In all our conversations, Bob never suggests that he answered Dave's letter.

Bob was particularly respected because of his worker status, even though he was younger than the rest of them. Of German-Christian descent, with an anarchist father who threw him out when he became a Communist, Bob was in awe of his young comrades who would have a discussion about anything. The majority were Jewish, and schooling meant a lot in their families. Bob remembers, "I got a phenomenal education just being part of that world, because I hadn't gone to school. I hadn't read anything. I didn't read books. There were discussions of Marx, of Freud, of Schubert. As well as, of course, our meetings that we would go over in minute detail afterwards."

Given the atmosphere among Dave's friends, all the talk of unemployment and Fascism, the worry about their parents in a new country and how hard it was to earn a living, as well as Dave's own personal conflicts, I wonder how he framed the question to himself about leaving. None of his close friends went to Spain. Only he. The single piece of evidence of a shared confidence was Bob's report to me, and he essentially rebuffed Dave. The boy may not have sought out anyone else's advice.

I'll never know what exactly pushed Dave to make his decision, but it is clear that his life in New York, at home, in school, and in the

YCL made him a man who might go. There was something unsatis-
fying and constricting, even dull and, at times, distressing about his
life. His parents moved from apartment to apartment during those
first ten years in America. They followed my grandfather's painting
jobs and the free rent in the buildings where he worked. Between
1927 and 1938, they lived in the Bronx, Washington Heights, Brooklyn, back in Washington Heights, and then back in the Bronx. Dave
began high school at George Washington in Washington Heights in
September 1930, but in January 1933, the family moved to Brooklyn
for a year. The following year, they went back to upper Manhattan.
Dave graduated from George Washington in June 1934.

According to his brother Phil, it was at New Utrecht High School
in Brooklyn that, in 1933, Dave encountered the American Communist Party and the YCL. He was eighteen. Unlike other groups of kids
hanging around outside of school, the YCL wasn't cliquish. They
welcomed new people. They invited you to hand out copies of the
Daily Worker with them and sometimes the *New Masses*, a political
and literary magazine. It was the Depression, and life was hard. But
distributing political literature, going to demonstrations, and arguing
intensely were fun.

Adolph Ross, who also knew Dave in Spain, was at New Utrecht
at the time. He told me that students were savvy there, aware, for
example, of Mussolini's rise to power at the end of the 1920s and his
bombing of Corfu in defiance of the League of Nations in 1923.
They organized a strike for peace, which attracted attention. "At that
time, we wanted to eliminate war," Ross tells me. "We were pacifists."

These kids had a keen sense of moral outrage, and they were not
shy. Ross recounts how they organized to get rid of their embezzling
principal. The students had to pay a fee for their student organization, and the principal was stealing from it. He also made the students
buy their lunches at school, forbidding them from leaving the prem-
ises. "He overcharged us and took the cream off the top," says Ross.
The students called a meeting of the parent-teacher organization and

presented their allegations. They contacted the press. "We were kids," says Ross, "but we were somebodies too. By the time we went to Spain, we already had political experience."

Dave probably fit in easily at New Utrecht, socially and politically. He was a person who liked to get things done. If he had a list of twenty students whom he wanted to persuade to demonstrate with his group, he surely spoke to each and every one of them. He was quiet spoken and reasonable. If he was talking to a girl, she might well have paid attention to and marveled at this unprepossessing boy, earnest and serious about politics but seemingly not interested in her romantically. And though she might have missed the flirtation, she enjoyed the respect. She relaxed in a way that was unusual with a boy.

Before Dave left New Utrecht, he got a letter of recommendation from the head of the German and Spanish Department. Dated January 30, 1934, it says, "To whom it may concern, This is to introduce David Lifshitz, a former member of this school, who has done outstanding work as captain of the German Office Squad. He is most intelligent and capable. I am sure you will find him very helpful and full of initiative, if you will give him an opportunity to show what he can do." After just one year at New Utrecht, he left with experiences he would depend on, and he was wise enough to ask for a letter attesting to his abilities.

George Washington High School, where he spent most of his high school years, was another milieu entirely. The writer Howard Fast, a student there in the late twenties, a working-class boy with street smarts, described it as "middle class, filled with well-dressed boys and girls who had allowances." The school had a drama club, modern literature club, psychology club, soccer team, service squad, and senior council. Dave's name appears in the high school yearbook alongside the words "Athlete, scholar an' everything. Soccer Team—Physics Club—Arista Chess Club—Cherry Tree Rep." Dave followed an academic program at George Washington, but his interests were clearly far ranging; he was on his way to becoming a complicated man. Further evidence of this is the fact that in his last year, Dave applied to the Baron de Hirsch Trade School to learn machine work. This school was part of the long arm of Jewish charity institutions established by the de Hirsch family. Clearly, being a conventionally rounded student wasn't all Dave wanted. Like so many young Communists, being a worker may have been Dave's ideal, but he wasn't of one mind. He was middle class in many of his appetites and Communist in his politics.

While Dave was attending George Washington, the family moved back to the South Bronx, to Crotona Boulevard. Soon after their arrival, my uncle Phil tells me, Dave headed over to the YCL headquarters on Tremont and Prospect. He discovered that in that area alone, there were three thousand members. When he graduated from high school in June 1934, he put his energy into the League full time. He tried to find paying jobs but had little luck. He was qualified at bookkeeping, and he could fix cars. He went to City College for a semester. The course he took was given at night at James Monroe High School in the Bronx, where my mother had gone to school. She probably helped him out, gave him pointers. He took one course in economics and then apparently dropped out.

I begin to get a sense of my mother and Dave. He was easy to be with, no yelling, no swagger, and just about her age. He shared his interest in Marxism with her. Maybe she gave him tips about girls and socializing, and maybe about dancing. She was a fabulous dancer too.

No one in the YCL seemed to know that Dave hadn't been born in the United States, that he in fact didn't become a citizen until 1937. People say his English was perfect. All are surprised to hear that he was born in Riga. As his brother Phil says, "Dave was Americanized." Maybe he made a special effort to fit in. Or perhaps he was secretive. In any case, Dave's European Jewishness was such a basic component of Communism in New York that his behavior and convictions were probably indistinguishable from those of others in the group. He was certainly one of the gang as he sat around chewing over political problems in cafeterias and automats, nursing a single cup of coffee for hours.

To Evelyn, my uncle was an American by the name of Dave Lipton. She didn't know that he spoke and wrote Yiddish fluently, as she did. She never heard him called "Duddy," his nickname in the family, or "Lifshitz," the name he graduated from high school with. Lifshitz changed to Lipton when he received his American citizenship in 1938.

Evelyn finds it unthinkable that Dave was called Duddy. He was far too serious for that. "We did a lot of dancing and singing in the YCL," Evelyn says, "and there was a lot of joking around at parties, but I can't see Dave as part of that. I remember him more sad than happy. He was troubled, I think." Pointing to the small photo of him I show her, in which he is smiling broadly with a male friend, she says, "This picture is very special. I don't remember him like that at all." She shrugs.

Finally, a whisper of some other Dave.

Some days, after a leadership training class, Dave walked Evelyn part of the way home across Bronx Park.

"Was he a gentleman?" I ask.

"Oh yes," she says quietly.

He would pull out a pack of cigarettes and light one. Then he'd ask her something related to the class. Had she understood "use-value" and "exchange-value"? Was the concept of "ideology" clear to her? He was the teacher. Phil once told me that Dave was going to be a teacher.

Evelyn enjoyed these walks. She found herself thinking bigger thoughts than usual. She felt safe with Dave but wondered that he never took her hand. She appreciated the respect he showed her and the seriousness with which he took her political education. She saw his intense concentration, how hard he worked thinking things through, trying to say them clearly. How honest he was. He never made her feel uncomfortable or nervous. She didn't understand why she felt calm with him, so at ease. "It's almost as if he wasn't a man, even though he was so good-looking," she says.

Evelyn remembers him pausing midsentence one day and turning his head in the direction of a grove of birch trees.

"Do you read poetry, Dave?" she asked.

"No, not really," he said. "Just what I had to in school. Why, you think I'm the poetic sort? Not tough enough, like some of the leaders?"

"No, I didn't mean that. There are just many lovely poems about nature. I thought you might enjoy them. That's all."

Bob Schrank says, "Young people who joined [our organization] came for the social life, but Dave was brooding and thinking all the time. At parties, he'd always be sitting quietly, talking in a corner. The guys would kid him about girls, and that made him blush."

Nobody links Dave to a girl romantically. Except my father. He says, "Girls loved him. What was not to love?" Phil disagrees: "He was withdrawn, passive, not involved with social activities, not assertive, not dating girls. Primarily he had men friends."

My grandmother may have fretted over the absence of girls in Dave's life. I did find several letters from girls in the shoebox. Summertime letters. Kids at camp or at hotels in the Catskills, working or with their families. There are a few awkward photographs of Dave with girls who look overbearing next to his shy self-containment. I can imagine Dave coming home one day and announcing to his mother—who is sitting at the dining-room table, reading the paper, a ritual often described by her sons—that he's decided to answer Marion, a girl he met the summer before at Banner Lodge. In a letter I've read, Marion asks him for some photo negatives he promised to send her. The hotel where they met is in Moodus, Connecticut, a town referred to as "the Catskills of Connecticut." The lodge itself is described as attracting "mostly Jewish vacationers. . . . [Jack Banner] had turned the farm started by his father Samuel 'Pop' Banner in 1922 into a popular summer destination. . . . [A] key to [its] success . . . was a thriving singles scene."

I find myself thinking again about those intimate photos of Dave with another man—let's call him Larry—one of the pictures whose playfulness startles Evelyn. The boys seem easy together, comfortable and indulgent. I can see them squeezing into a photo booth in the subway, kidding around, mugging for the camera, Larry more wholeheartedly than Dave perhaps.

Evelyn suspects things about Dave that she takes her time to volunteer. She tells me that she saw in his *farkrimpte ponim*, as she puts it—his contorted face—something twisted, unhappy. In a letter she sent to my father after Dave's death, she wrote, "He gave me understanding in many things and the mere fact that he was moody, and had . . . things wrong with him, like any normal person, taught me a great deal."

When I ask what she meant by those words, she says she can't remember. But she senses that there was much about Dave she didn't know. He rarely told her anything personal. She was seven years younger, she says. Sometimes something would slip out, though. She thinks there was a problem with a brother, with Lou.

When I send her a copy of her letter to my father, she's taken aback. "Why did I write to him?" she asks. "I knew they didn't get on." Except for Dave's comments in his letter from Spain to my father, I've never heard that they didn't get along. I ask my father about this.

"She's got it wrong." He's fidgeting on the other end of the line. "What does she know? All those years ago. People don't remember straight. They get things confused."

"Well, that's what she said."

"Look, I loved my brother," he says. "Don't make a mountain out of a molehill."

Evelyn remembers something more about Lou, something about

a letter she thinks he sent to Spain, something about mocking Dave's political involvement, and something about girls. Probably some girl Louis didn't approve of, Evelyn thinks. Louis was said to be quite the lady's man. Maybe the girl was fat or something, she says.

Eddy Meskin, who became the YCL membership director for Bronx County in the late 1930s and subsequently worked for the United Office and Professional Workers of America, remembers going to the pier to say good-bye to Dave and the other guys who were leaving for Spain. "You couldn't wave or anything," he says. "It was secret." Eddy also mentions a letter from Louis. "It's a sad story, Dave's," he says. "He had trouble with a brother, and it apparently made it hard for him in Spain. I don't know how exactly. But people say Dave never got any mail, except one letter at the beginning. We heard that from several comrades who were with him. I mean, when people didn't get mail, they could chalk it up to the war, the bad conditions, but most of the guys got *some* mail. They say that after that first letter, Dave didn't receive anything. I know he wrote home. I'd occasionally run into his brother Lou, and he'd say Dave was doing fine, but I guess Louis never wrote to him again. Dave also had a sister-in-law who really loved him, that was obvious. She collected money for the brigade, I remember, on the subway, even though she was on crutches with a broken leg. How come she didn't write? He never got a letter or a package from anyone. And the mother, she was a real supporter of the party. Some say he snapped over there. Still, I know he did a good job. The Vet who spoke at his memorial was explicit about that."

Dave never received any mail! I don't understand. I have the letters he wrote, those fragile pieces of lined paper with English and Yiddish words carefully spelled out across them. Those letters are the hardest evidence of a living, breathing, hopeful—and anxious—Dave. Naturally, I've assumed they were answered, that he had the company of friends and family in Spain and knew that his parents had forgiven him, knew he was still loved. Those words at the end of the first letter he sent to his parents: "[F]orgive me, understand me and please don't be angry." Now people are telling me that the letters weren't answered. Instantly, I know this is true. I don't know how I know, but I do. Maybe I've sensed something in my father's jumpy responses to my questions, what often seemed like a string of non sequiturs, which I took to be his self-absorbed habit of always bringing things back to himself. Now it occurs to me that perhaps his peculiar sentence structures resulted from his hiding something.

I sit down with Dave's letters again. Once more, I peruse that first one to his parents, in which he informs them that he is in Spain and apologizes to them for lying. He says at the end,

> Write often, every week and send packages when you can. . . . I don't know how long I will remain here. Don't worry. Don't worry. I can take care of myself. Let me know how you are. How's Trudy, Philip, Louis and all the rest. Be well and don't be angry, Salud! Duddy. I just reminded myself that July 18th is my birthday and the best present I can get from you is a letter of your forgiveness and love.

I reread the letters, and now find that in each one, he asks, "Write soon and often." "Write often, every week and send packages when you can." On August 10, ten days before he was shot, Dave wrote, "Have not heard from the States yet." Could he possibly explain this absence to himself by the slow mail service? No letters from Louis, Phil, Trudy, his parents? Some long-buried bitterness might have plowed its way up through him then, some suspicion about his brothers, some shame related to his parents. His mother could get angry. Maybe it was that he had hurt them—even betrayed them by leaving—and they had turned against him. Such thoughts could have heightened the scorching heat of the Spanish days, the frigid cold of the nights, the fear, and the terrible, terrible waiting.

Still, Dave must have made friends there. It troubles me, though, that the only group picture I have that includes him is from the Battle of the Ebro, and the boys and men who look American are ranged on the left, while Dave sits on the right amid older Spanish-looking men with berets. A heartbreaking sobriety stares out of each man's face, with an occasional smirk cracking the surface. It is as if they are saying, Why bother photographing us? We'll all be dead in no time.

So here was this amiable, easygoing fellow—whom some found melancholy but who was liked and wept over even sixty years after his death—and none of them wrote to him? My father could be a harsh and heartless man, but I always hoped that in an extreme situation when the stakes couldn't be higher, his heart would unclench, and he'd smile, open his arms, and say, "Just kidding. Sure, I'll be there. I'm coming right over." That man would have written to his brother. Wouldn't he have? But then, how can I understand my father's obsessively repeated phrases? "Mind your own business." "He died for nothing." "He threw his life away."

I suppose it could have been my father's broken heart speaking, but truly, I don't know how to figure my father's love for his brother. Was I mistaken to think that it was love when he took the box down from the closet—all that attention and reverie? And the box's contents bespoke my father's attachment to Dave and Spain, didn't they? But the iconic phrases and ritualized gestures didn't feel now like signs of emotions so much as fetishized responses that masked something else, something unmanageable and wayward. Maybe my father didn't love Dave *because* he went to Spain and died there. Rather, he loved him *before* he went. He loved the young man they all did, the "angel," the sweetheart, the person who looked you in the eye, the man who listened.

Wouldn't my father have been more respectful of Dave's memory if it had been his death that shattered him? And might not his feelings, in that case, have been more complicated and the expression of them more nuanced?

these step off the pages of Anzia Yezierska's *Bread Givers*, Henry Roth's *Call It Sleep*, Paule Marshall's *Brown Girl, Brownstones.*

My grandmother held the family in a firm grip. In fact, much has been made of the overbearing Jewish mother. "When [she] worried about her little boy going down to play," writes Irving Howe, "it was not merely the dangers of Rivington or Cherry Street that she saw . . . it was the streets of Kishinev and Bialystok and other towns in which the blood of Jewish children had been spilled. Later, such memories would fade among those she had meant to shield and it would become customary to regard her as a grotesque figure of excess." I wonder who my grandmother was to Dave.

Anxiety, paranoia, and class anger marked many families, immigrant and otherwise, in early and mid-twentieth-century America. Working-class people all over the country became socialists, Communists, and anarchists in the 1930s. At least one son or daughter might look out at a ravaged America, dream of changing things, and then work to do just that. The optimism that looks so forced to us now, that beamed out of Soviet posters, was what many young American leftists were searching for. Perhaps that was the lure for Dave—hopefulness and realizable goals. Such optimism could organize his life and calm him, and at the same time it could nourish the seeds of a dream to be elsewhere. His favorite book was Maxim Gorky's *Mother*, whose Communist hero, Pavel, expresses sentiments that are tinny to our ears today: "A new heart's being born to life. Man is striding ahead . . . calling as he goes: 'People of all lands, unite in one family!'" But to many an American immigrant during and just after the Great Depression, those words weren't corny. The revolution in Russia seemed nothing less than a miracle. And Jews hoped to find a welcoming place in that revolution where there had never been one before. They might not have been accepted as Russians, but they could be accepted, they hoped, as Soviets and comrades. The appeal of this universal equality to a pariah people was mighty. An impressionable, out-of-work boy like Dave, with a

Communist-leaning family history, leapt at Communism in America. He was right at home.

Dave found among Communists familiar European faces and accents, insouciant shrugs, and self-deprecating jokes. There were bagels, knishes, and salami sandwiches. *And* there were American Christians like Bob Schrank and Bill Wheeler. I knew my father's card-playing buddies and Miami pals, and none of them bore the slightest resemblance to Bill Wheeler. For one thing, there wasn't a Christian person among them.

Whatever the reason, Dave chose Bill. On the boat, in Paris, then in the Sierra Pandols. He confided in him that he'd never slept with a woman. He gave him a letter high up in the barren mountains; the next day, he took it back and tore it up in front of his friend. When a bullet found him, he was talking to Bill. As the bullet's force pushed him forward, he lurched toward Bill, a man as exotic as any a Lipton had ever seen.

Bill had grown up on a farm in Columbia County, New York. His mother, he told me, was born in a sod hut in Manhattan, Kansas. Her family had been on their way to California when they decided to stay in Kansas. Even Bill admits that he thinks the Communist Party sent him home to raise money for Spain because he looked American.

"As in, not Jewish or black?" I ask.

"I think so," he replies.

"I am not proud of being an American," Bill later reveals to me. "A book that had a great influence on me when I was a boy was *Westward Ho!* by Charles Kingsley. It started with the Inquisition and the torture of Jews and continued to the conquest of the Americas and the Indians. It was then that I became an atheist. I was about fourteen when I read it. I hated what this country did to the Indians. And slavery. I hated it."

It takes me aback to hear Bill talk about America in this way. I never felt American myself growing up, nor did anyone in my family. We were Jews, left-wingers, New Yorkers. There was always criticism of the United States, a litany about the degradation of workers, the too-high regard for men like Ford, Rockefeller, Carnegie, the lack of respect for older people, the dirty streets and flavorless food, the racism. But there we were in America, enthralled by the skyscrapers and movie houses, the free schools and libraries, the ballparks and parade of shiny gadgets. And the steaks, the bacon, the hot dogs, the hamburgers, secretly scarfed down out of sight of our families. Not to mention the freedom to be Jewish, not to be religious but simply to *be*. The security to live that identity without fear. Still, it was normal in my progressive immigrant home to criticize America. Bill, on the other hand, struck me as such an American. I wasn't prepared for this critique from him.

My father never said anything one way or the other about America. But I got the impression that it didn't matter much to him. Where he was didn't matter. In most cases, whom he was with didn't either. You could say my father was excessive about independence. He once told me that you had to make sure the car you owned didn't get the upper hand. "Don't get too attached," he'd say, "you know, cleaning it all the time, keeping it shiny. It has to know who's boss." He made the same point about the chocolates and pastries in his parents' shop in Riga. "You have to eat to live, not live to eat," he told me proudly. A piece of chocolate could get the upper hand with my father.

In Hurleyville, I remember someone mentioning the hotel down the road that had a sign in front of it: "No dogs or Jews."

"Ach," my father said, "who cares?"

"You don't care about anything," snapped Grandma. He never answered her back. No, he wouldn't care about anything. It was a principle with him. I remember something about his not wanting to fight in World War II and getting out of it somehow. Maybe that childhood experience in Riga had unhinged him more than he admitted.

"Is that what brought you to the party, Bill?" I ask. "That you weren't proud of being an American?"

"No," he replies. "That wasn't it. I was looking for answers." He was on his way, at seventeen, to being a farmer, he tells me. On his mother's suggestion, he attended an agricultural school in Cobbleskill, New York. He had a good time there, generally hanging out with older people. But times were changing, he says. It was toward the end of the 1920s, and the large farm families of eighteen children were shrinking. People were leaving for the cities. He met an older woman who suggested that he come to New York with her, and at seventeen, that's what he did.

"Just like that?" I ask.

"Yeah, I was biding my time. Why not go?"

Unfortunately, when they got to New York, she took up with a former boyfriend, and Bill was left in a small apartment on Eleventh Street east of Third Avenue, more or less alone. She had introduced him, though, to a politically progressive world. "During that period, I met a number of people who had a great influence on me," he says. "One was an ironworker on a high-rise, a fellow by the name of Carpenter, a big tough guy and an old Wobbly, you know, a member of the IWW," the Industrial Workers of the World. "A great guy. He never got hurt up at the top, but he did get drunk once and was hit by a car. I visited him in the hospital while his ribs were healing, and we'd have very illuminating political discussions. He was educating me.

"Then there was a taxi driver by the name of Abe Moscow. He was a Communist. We used to take long walks, and he gave me a political education too. I must have been eighteen or nineteen years old. We were strolling down Madison Avenue one night, and two cops chased us. That made me furious. Abe used that as an object lesson of the role of the police in the State. These people were very honest and sincere. They really impressed me."

Bill's mother was able to find him a job driving a truck for a man who had a health-food store and who also ferried people from the city to a leftist camp in Shelton, New Jersey. It was at that camp that

Bill met his first wife, a Hungarian woman who was three years older than he and, in his words, "about thirty years more sophisticated." Through her father and with the financial help of the owner of the health-food store, Bill went to Russia for two years, from 1932 to 1934. He was in his early twenties.

"Why did you go?" I ask.

"I was excited, for one thing, because it was the first time I had been out of the country. And, as I told you, I was looking for answers. People were emphatic about their beliefs about the Soviet Union in those days. I wanted to find out for myself. Also I was hating walking the streets hungry, grateful if somebody in a greasy spoon gave me something to eat when I washed a few dishes. Grateful for what? In the Soviet Union, I learned what could be. Free education, health care, good housing for everybody. I met a man who was fifty-five years old, a plumber, who was accepted into the university, and he was going to be paid a stipend to go! That impressed me. I thought I wanted to be a writer then."

Few people in the States knew at that time how Stalin accomplished his megalomaniacal goals. Certainly not the foot soldiers of the party, like Dave and his friends and Bill. What if Bill had been aware that the years he was in the USSR coincided with the height of the Ukrainian famine, which killed six to eight million people and was caused not by nature but by Stalin's forced collectivization of farms? What if Dave had read what I had by the Russian Communist Isaac Babel, who rode with the Red Cavalry into Poland in 1920 and confided to his diary: "Same old story . . . the Jews have been plundered . . . they expected the Soviet regime to liberate them, and suddenly there were shrieks, whips cracking, shouts of 'dirty Yid.' . . . We are the vanguard, but of what? The population await their saviors, the Jews look for liberation—and in ride the Kuban Cossacks." Who knows what would have become of Dave or Bill if one had gone to the Soviet Union and the other had stayed there?

Bill was looking for social and political answers in Communism. He arrived there via anarchism, the Wobblies, and socialism. For Dave, Communism was politics drenched in the smells of his mother's kitchen as much as the secrecy and excitement surrounding the comings and goings in Riga of his uncles Dovid and Shloime. These politics may have represented a boyhood wish to be with them, and with his mother, a way of being "home." And yet a way out too.

Certainly, when the Lifshitz boys came to New York, they carried their uncles' politics with them. My father tried a course in Marxism. Phil belonged to a Marxist discussion group in the hospital where he interned. It was Dave, though, who threw himself completely into political work. He translated his European past into a new life in America. He developed his own narrative, in his own way, that was separate from his mother's, his uncles', and his brothers'.

I ask Bill how he felt about my uncle being Jewish.

"We didn't dwell on such things," he says. But then he adds, "Come to think of it, maybe I went to Spain because of my Jewish friends, what Hitler was doing to the Jews."

For Dave's part, what a relief it might have been to have this friend whose family was Christian. To know where he ended and where his friend began, not taking each other's emotional pulse every two minutes, not having the intensity and over-familiarity that so often happens among Jews. What bracing clarity this could have been.

One day, I wonder aloud to Bill if there weren't things about America that he loved.

"Well," he replies, "I was eight when the armistice was signed at the end of World War I, and I remember feeling that now I never will be able to fight for my country. I must have felt some love. I must have grown up with that. But you know, in Spain I felt I was fighting for principles that I thought were right for everyone. . . . My comrades were the best men and women I've ever known. Many people have said to me, you know, you claim to be an atheist but you're a better person than any of the Christians I know. That's what my comrades were like: good people."

Here was Bill with his American Protestant roots, Dave an immigrant Jew, Bill growing up on a farm, Dave in a cosmopolitan northern European city, then New York. One came from solid, down-to-earth farmers and workers of few words, the other from a highly combative verbal tradition. But they both believed in the promise of social revolution. And in Spain.

My father laughed at them. Revolution, sure! I could hear him gloating. But maybe, after all, there were days when he stopped, amazed at and envious of their optimism and commitment, their sticking to ideals and working hard to accomplish them. Maybe Dave surprised him too, when he stepped into tense tenant situations that brought the police running. Or when he organized street demonstrations, whipped up emotions in front of nonunionized stores, or even just handed out the *Daily Worker*.

My father never experienced such a pull in his life, except perhaps toward playing the stock market, which he did while at the same time criticizing American capitalism. He sold his furniture store when he was fifty-nine, spending his time afterward reading and playing chess mostly against himself, in geographical locations he changed every six months. He moved from La Jolla to Miami to Netanya, Israel, and back to Miami again, until he was eighty-five or so. Then he stayed in Israel, where he never learned Hebrew and never stopped complaining. His restlessness may have been his way of going home again. After all, his parents moved from Latvia to the United States, then back and forth from one borough to another in New York, and finally to the Catskills. I think my father died more or less contented. He was insulated from life's bigger questions by his doting second wife, the enervating heat of the places where he lived, and his increasing age. Not exactly Al Pacino nodding off in a lawn chair in Corleone, Sicily, but close.

Bill and Dave couldn't have been brothers, but they suited each other. They were easygoing, with a touch of the French about them as they regarded you, bemused but taking you in. Both were slim and lithe. They were optimists and activists, and they shared a certain passivity as well. They didn't mind other people telling them what to do. Both were close to their mothers. From what I learned from Evelyn and my own mother, Dave, like Bill, took women seriously.

It was Bill's mother who helped him off the farm, first encouraging him to study agriculture, then introducing him to the right people in the city when he needed a job. Bill remembers that she "was always very active in whatever she took up. In the Grange, a farmer's organization, she was involved in developing methods of canning fruits and vegetables. She lectured on home economics too." He adds, "My father was never a farmer. He worked in the city as a mechanic. Earlier, in England, where he was born, he invented machinery that made net stockings for women and the gauges for setting the needles on hosiery machines. That saved the company millions of dollars. For this, they gave him a pat on the back and a five-dollar-a-week raise. It wasn't right, the way they treated him." Bill continues, smiling nervously, "My father was a hard man with a heavy hand, and my bottom felt it very often."

My dad recalls ruefully that when his father came to New York, he no longer dressed in handsome suits and ties the way he had in Riga. The vests and long sweaters my grandpa wore, which I found friendly and inviting, were a mark of failure in my father's eyes, and perhaps in Dave's too. I don't think my grandpa cared. He wasn't a businessperson. Maybe he never liked formal dress. Grandma was the one with the head for figures and profit. She might have been a Communist, but she was quite bourgeois.

Bill loved his father, and I'm sure that Dave loved Grandpa. I know my father did. His eyes teared up when he remembered his father, although I never knew what he was remembering or what the tears meant. I found it baffling that his cocky style made as much room for Grandpa as it did. I remember my grandfather waving good-bye to us in Hurleyville, weeping, a sturdy man in his winter coat and felt Borsalino. My father said that Grandpa was dominated by Grandma, but maybe he sensed the love between them and envied it. My grandfather was a confident and serene man. Surely Louis would have liked to have some of that.

Dave probably looked to Grandpa for solace, as others did, but he may have been held tight by Grandma, something of the mama's boy, perhaps the closest person to the daughter she never had. He was her baby, her Benjamin, the only one to have her fair coloring. I was aware of nighttime disturbances in Hurleyville when I was a child, my normally imperturbable grandma sobbing in the night. That would have been just six years after Dave disappeared without a trace.

I have seen pictures in which Bill looks androgynous. He equivocates; he withdraws. There's no leap in his body. It's all rest and waiting. There's a Spanish Civil War poster behind him in one picture. He's in a dark, tightly fitted suit, a shirt checkered like large-square graph paper, a silk tie. He grasps the side of a chair, his face in profile. Maybe this picture was taken when he returned from Spain in 1937 to raise money for the Spanish Republic. His face is a boy's, or a plain girl's, a pure girl's, eyes downcast, tender, and ungendered, hair swept up and off his forehead like the lift of angel wings. His contemplation is deep, like that of an artist considering his palette. Dave looks like this in one of the little subway photos I have of him, in which he seems to be playing revolutionary.

Bill sometimes appears in photos with his hips thrust forward, like a sculpture of Adonis or like tough boys on the streets all over the United States, a pose of imperviousness, as he does in a photograph with Canadian volunteer Jack Steel. Except with Bill, there's a lapse. His head and neck push forward, and his mouth too. There's something

needy about him. This would have embarrassed my father. It's one reason he would never have been drawn to Bill, a man who seemed boyish even at eighty-seven. When I see Bill in photographs, I sense that in his personal life, he never went beyond this hesitancy. It wrapped him in benevolence.

What men like my father would call weakness in Bill—his uncertainty and curiosity—was strength. Those qualities made him resilient and evenhanded. What daring it took to be a man like that, and what confidence. My father might have found him neither assertive nor cocksure enough, but there was Bill at twenty-five, an officer in a foreign war. My father had been sufficiently fearful that even in the face of Nazism, he wouldn't enlist in the American army.

"I grew up in Spain," Bill says. "I learned that I wasn't easily frightened, that I could take it. Dave was a good boy. He didn't complain. He was in full command of himself. He wasn't overly concerned, although you had the sense he was measuring himself, but he was not overly frightened or anything of that sort." Perhaps Bill saw something of himself in my uncle, sensed the struggle in him between longing and ambivalence, an emotionally littered path Dave navigated cautiously.

Whatever else happened in Spain, Bill worries that he failed Dave, that he didn't call out fast enough—and the boy crumpled at his feet, the letter never sent. "I can still see the look on his face," Bill says. I wonder if he in fact was, for a split second, just happy to see Dave at that instant and therefore torn between wanting to relax in a normal way, as perhaps they had done in Paris, and warning him to get down and protect himself. Bill had also unwittingly complicated Dave's destiny in his family by colluding with him in destroying that last letter. After all, when Bill first accepted the letter from Dave, he had said, joking with him but also perhaps mildly critical, "You will make it O.K. Just keep your head and fanny down." These words and Bill's imagined negligence at the very last moment might well have preyed on his mind for the rest of his life.

Bill grows silent. Dave trusted him, confided in him. Why didn't Dave give the letter to Ben Katine, the friend he knew from the Bronx? Perhaps it was that Bill was the commander of the company, and Dave hoped that his authority would make him impervious, that somehow Bill would survive, that he would be there afterward. Maybe Dave thought he'd jinx himself if his old friend Ben knew his fears. Maybe Dave didn't want Ben to know about his altercation with Lou. Perhaps there was something about that in the letter. And Bill already knew things about Dave. It was clean and clear with Bill, not messy, not like home.

Dave stood before Bill, sweet tempered and solid, never talking too much, never through his hat the way some did. "He didn't have any sharp edges," Bill says.

Even when Bill is old, it doesn't seem so, or it doesn't matter. I know that his manner has always been the same. This unprepossessing man stretches across decades, even as he sits so lightly on the earth. He is an ordinary man and satisfied with that. Neither suspicion nor cunning contorts his face or narrows his eyes. Only his honesty and self-containment could be construed as seductive. And his gentleness. Dave could have loved him, a man like that.

6

WHY?

DURING A LULL in battle, a soldier in his twenties asks an older volunteer, "Why did you come to Spain? You have a wife and kids. Why did you come?" This is the question the Vets are asked more than any other. It turns out that they even ask each other. And of course, it is my question too. Why those men, those women, my uncle?

A good boy was meant to do his duty, earn a living, share expenses, respect his parents. Dave wrote to his mother and father, "Please excuse me for what I wrote earlier, about working in a hotel. It was all a lie, a way to comfort you, to avoid having you hate me for the anguish I caused you. When I return from Spain to you, I will tell you the whole story and ask for your forgiveness." He was a loyal son. His decision couldn't have been easy.

Passion and desire drove them. As did orneriness and frustration with their lives. For most, regardless of each one's particular emotional profile, politics got them up every morning. Many have said that the volunteers were an extremely sophisticated group of people politically. They leapt the parameters of what should have been their destiny and became the people they longed to be. But desire has always been, and will always be, a slippery urge to track.

It is difficult to appreciate to what extent Communism was, in its origins, the great-grandchild of the Enlightenment and the ideals of the French Revolution: Liberty, Equality, Fraternity; reason, not faith; government by law. Reasonable Europeans on the left and right today respect those positions, whatever their disagreements with Communism as political practice, and even though its theories, at their best, have long since become mere shouting points in political debates. The positive marks that Communism (Marxism, really) in the form of democratic socialism has left in the laws of even conservative countries—more equitable distribution of wealth and the rights of human beings to decent housing, health care, unemployment insurance, and old-age security—are seen as a just response to capitalism.

In the 1930s in America, for those who were inspired by the hope Communism represented and the strategies it proposed, political commitment trumped everything, including family. As Vivian Gornick put it, those who believed in Communism "remade the family in the image of workers all over the world." My brother used this language when he condemned our uncle's departure for Spain. "Why the Cause," he asked, "and not the family? To give your life for a great cause or for humanity is easy. But to support your family, to support one person you love throughout his life, that's what's tough. He betrayed his family. He didn't get a job, he ran away."

You were born into your family, but you chose your comrades. For Dave and Bill and Evelyn, the party meant everything. You went to meetings and demonstrations. You participated in study groups. You helped the evicted and the unemployed. You marched on picket lines. You went to Spain. In the 1930s, these were American as well as Communist impulses.

Communism itself Americanized in that decade. By the mid-1930s, its ideology overlapped with that of Roosevelt's New Deal. Both were anti-Fascist and anti–monopoly capitalism. Goals for both were economic recovery and, importantly, relief for the unemployed and impoverished. Among Communists in America, words like "progressive" and "democracy" replaced "proletarian" and "dictatorship of the proletariat." A party slogan became "Communism is the Americanism of the twentieth century."

Nonetheless, those who went to Spain were intoxicated by the thought that they were the first international working-class army. "We were an army of civilians," Steve Nelson, a beloved education commissar said. "We weren't drafted." In 1939, Alvah Bessie, a writer who in 1950 would be imprisoned and blacklisted for refusing to name names to the House Un-American Activities Committee, wrote, "We were proud of our army. It was a People's Army, drawing its strength from the people's will to resist oppression." The artist Ben Gardner wrote to his girlfriend from Spain: "I with other American comrades had the honor to be on guard duty at night . . . the wonderful feeling of holding a rifle with bayonet, guarding Democracy. For the first time in my life I felt that it is not capitalist property I'm guarding . . . but the property of the workers, the people of Spain."

When Bessie arrived in Spain in the spring of 1938, about the same time Dave did, the internationalism thrilled him. New recruits were welcomed in Albacete in a courtyard hung with flags from Great Britain, France, America, the Soviet Union, Czechoslovakia, Finland, Norway, the Irish Free State, Cuba. Europeans spoke three, four, and five languages. Newspapers from all over the world lay around the camp. Soldiers sang "The Internationale," "La Marseillaise," "Casey Jones," "Freiheit."

Between December 1936 and September 1938, 2,800 American men and women went to Spain, the majority illegally. People originated in fifty-two different countries. Germans and Italians formed, according to American volunteer and historian Robert Colodny, "the hard core of the International columns . . . their countries [having already] gone down to defeat by the fascists." Battalions were named after national heroes: the Garibaldi Battalion after Giuseppe Garibaldi, the champion of Italian liberation and unification; the Thaelmann after German Communist Party leader Ernst Thaelmann. The George Washington and Abraham Lincoln battalions merged into one near the end of the war and became known as the Abraham Lincoln Brigade. As Peter Carroll, a historian of the brigade, once said to me, a majority of the Americans' "ancestors were not Abraham Lincolns, but they named their battalions after patriotic heroes." They were proud to be Americans.

Volunteers came from every state in the Union except Delaware and Wyoming. They were workers, intellectuals, clerks, artists, lawyers, doctors, nurses, secretaries, sailors, autoworkers, longshoremen. Carroll writes that "most of the volunteers were blue-collar workers—seamen, drivers and mechanics were the most frequently listed occupations." Some were educated, but most hadn't finished high school. They were the first fully integrated battalion in American history, with more than eighty African American volunteers. Oliver Law, one of them, briefly became commander in the spring of 1937. Over a third were Jews. Among the women, the vast majority of whom were nurses, more than half were Jewish. Carroll notes that many of the American volunteers had been born in Europe. They were first-generation immigrants, which perhaps made them sensitive to the struggles of people in other parts of the world. It wasn't unimaginable to leave the place where you lived if you had already done that.

Eighty American women went. Black, white, and Asian, single and married, with children and without. Before she left for Spain, Salaria Kee, a black nurse, wanted to work with the American Red Cross to help flood victims in her native Ohio. "They told me they had no place for me. That the color of my skin would make me more trouble than I'd be worth." A friend suggested Spain to her, and that's where she went. "I didn't even know I was black there," she remembered when she was older.

Lini Fuhr, a graduate student in public health and a mother, wrote, "I felt I *had* to go to play my little part toward shaping a decent world."

Ruth Davidow, a nurse, declared, "[I] was politicized my whole life," but it had been Roosevelt's position of neutrality that tipped the scales for her. "I only cared," she told an interviewer, "when Mussolini and Hitler went in to help Spain, and I realized they wanted everything, the whole world, not a piece here and a piece there."

Letters home were filled with responses to the question "Why?" They were addressed to parents especially, but to lovers too. Hyman Katz, a teacher, wrote to his mother:

> Together with their agent, Franco, [Mussolini and Hitler] are try-
> ing to set up the same anti-progressive, anti-Semitic regime in
> Spain, as they have in Italy and Germany. . . . Realizing this, can I
> sit by and wait until the beasts get to my very door? . . . [A]s a
> Jew and a progressive, I would be among the first to fall under
> the ax of the fascists. . . . So I took up arms against the persecu-
> tors of my people—the Jews—and my class—the Oppressed.

Peter Frye, born in Montreal and one of the Vets who had been active in the left-wing theater movement in New York, told an inter-viewer that after seeing some pictures in a newspaper depicting events in Spain, he said to himself, "I can't live in this world if I don't fight against this." Canute Frankson, an African American autoworker from Detroit, wrote to a friend:

> On the battlefields of Spain we fight for the preservation of
> democracy. Here, we're laying the foundation for world peace,
> and for the liberation of my people, and of the human race. Here,
> where we're engaged in one of the most bitter struggles of
> human history, there is no color line, no discrimination, no race
> hatred. There's only one hate, and that is the hate for fascism.

John Cookson, a student at the University of Wisconsin, wrote to his aunt that "all of these things which I submitted myself to voluntarily, as have 3,000 other Americans, are . . . no[t] for any adventurism . . . they can be but for one thing—to follow the bright star of your beliefs to the bitter end, though it be death itself."

My uncle wrote to his parents on July 10, 1938:

> Now, you will ask me why did you go. If everybody tried to talk me out of it, why did I go. Here's why: Dear Mom and Pop, if you would be in Spain now and you would see what I see you would understand why I came here. If you would see hundreds of children poverty-stricken, ripped apart and shot to pieces, without parents, bloated from hunger, hundreds of mothers grieving, wild with fear, torn with grief, with their men taken from them and shot. . . . You would understand why I came here to help them.

Maury Colow, a Vet who after the war organized for the Congress of Industrial Organizations (the CIO) in Chicago, told filmmaker Judith Montell, "We were radicalized by social conditions"—poverty, the inescapable signs of inequality, the indifference of the rich. People wanted to work but couldn't find jobs, like Bill Wheeler, who practically had to beg for food. "It was humiliating," Bill told me. Davidow described seeing her first Hoovervilles, with people living in cardboard boxes and pieces of tin in Brooklyn near her house. These people looked just like her and her family. In Spain, she said, people were fighting against evil, but in the United States, they could do little to defend themselves. "We learned in Spain to act, not just to talk," she explained. Steve Nelson agreed: "We got to the point where [we felt,] enough of loafing and thinking, now it's time to act."

A remarkably high percentage of the men and women who went to Spain from America had grown up in orphanages, placed there often temporarily by impoverished parents. Harry Fisher, an easygoing, thoughtful man who became a runner in Spain, was one such person. He told me that he learned about bullies in an orphanage near Yonkers. He couldn't stand people like that, he said. He also learned about love in the orphanage. In a fragment of an unpublished memoir called "Caring," Fisher wrote, "We played together, we had our disagreements and fights, we were beaten by bullies, we were hungry together. Yes, we suffered and had good times—we laughed and we cried. And most important, we cared for one another."

Bullies and friendship were what Harry found when he joined the picket line to support the Department Store Employees Union in New York. That's where he made lifelong friendships. Workers and their friends were fighting the same inequalities that had forced many of their parents to institutionalize them as children. They were eager to defend the rights of workers at department stores like Klein's and Orbach's in New York. Harry and his wife, Ruthie, worked for TASS, the Russian news agency, into the early 1990s. Harry was so engaged politically that he died of a heart attack immediately after marching in a demonstration against the Iraq war, on March 22, 2003. He was ninety-two years old.

Harry's closest friends all his life were the people with whom he went to Spain. Johnny Murra was one of them. Murra saved Harry's life in Spain. After the war, he became a celebrated anthropologist. Jack Shafran, a New York contractor, was another lifelong friend of Harry's. They knew each other from Brooklyn, from before the war. They'd been in jail together when they were still in their teens for picketing with department-store workers. Normie Berkowitz was part of the same circle. All were activists in the Local 1250 of the Department Store Employees Union.

I've watched Harry and Jack and Normie sit side by side at Abraham Lincoln Brigade reunions, their bodies easy together, trusting. These men belie clichés of what a man is supposed to be, especially men who were volunteer soldiers. They leave each other room, they listen, they are tender with one another. I can see Dave next to them.

But not my father, who would always be looking over his shoulder trying to spot the next person in line ready to take advantage of him. He says he should have gone to Spain, but he couldn't have. He might have envied his brother's commitment, but it didn't really entice him.

Certainly, some of the men who went were like my father—vain, paranoid, defensive—but they were in the minority. Mostly I met fine people with grand ideals. Bill told me, "We were all pacifists." Harry Fisher agreed: "The Vets hated war. One day in Spain, Dave Reed [sic] said to me, 'You know I can't believe I'm leading men into battle, I who only knew about war by being in anti-war demonstrations. And I'm leading men whose only experience is the same.'" Harry lowered his head and murmured, "Dave Reed [sic] died that afternoon." Bill, who came so close to becoming a farmer alongside his parents, says, "I loved farming, but I hated butchering." James Lardner, the son of writer Ring Lardner, wrote to his mother, "If it is any comfort to you at all, I still hate violence and cruelty and suffering."

Colow, who was expelled from the Communist Party in 1952 for his irreverence, and who in 1956 became executive secretary of the VALB, expressed his philosophy eloquently in Montell's *Forever Activists*. "The most beautiful thing in life," he told her, "is when you're living not for yourself but outside of yourself and doing things that have more impact than on your own life." Milt Wolff, an art student when he left for Spain, where he became the last commander of the brigade at twenty-three years old, said, "To be a bystander is to participate in the criminality."

Way up through the 1990s, when they were in their eighties and nineties, these men and women visited schools, talked to students, lectured at libraries and galleries. Bill Bailey, a merchant seaman who spoke a working-class English with a thick Irish accent, told a classroom of high school kids in Spain, "Become part of something." Sam Gonshak, who, like my uncle, had been involved in the Unemployed Councils, emerged in Spain as a political commissar, and later in

New York he became the commander of the New York office of the VALB. He said, "If you give up, you're going to have a wilderness in this world." By the 1980s, most of them didn't talk about Communism. They would not allow what the Soviets made of Communism in Russia to throw a pall over their own politics or to ruin their history in Spain. They wanted Americans to know about the Spanish Civil War and about Americans' role in it.

Many of the men had never shot a gun when they left for Spain. Training was uneven. Alvah Bessie wrote:

> We marched and counter-marched . . . we trotted and ran;
> we ran and fell with our rifles, learning how to fall without hurt-
> ing ourselves . . . we practiced infiltration over the terrain—
> advancing by squads and platoons and sections; seeking cover,
> advancing, charging. We dug various types of fortifications—
> fox-holes, firing-pits, dugouts and trenches, and we learned how
> to camouflage them. We received instruction in musketry. . . .

Bill told me that he taught riflery in Spain. He knew about guns from growing up on a farm.

But then you read the following in Dr. John Simon's diary of February and March 1937:

> Yesterday the boys in the battalion had a meeting because of the
> bloody defeat they suffered when they went over the top. A
> commandant gave them an official story, explaining why things
> came off badly. . . . He said they would have rest—two days in
> Morata when they could wash. Then they laughed. Then the
> boys took the floor—I've never heard anything like it. Boys were
> crying because they didn't know how to use their rifles. The
> machine-gunner broke into tears as he explained how the guns

wouldn't work, how they were not properly equipped. One soldier explained how a boy went over the top with full equipment—and died.

Abe Osheroff, a carpenter with philosophical, literary, and filmmaking skills, volunteered when he was twenty-one. He admitted in 1984, irony tripping across his smile, "We were a bunch of kids, eighteen- and nineteen-year-olds. Our commander was twenty-three!"

Here's how Harry Fisher described his first day in battle: "I began to think all the wrong thoughts. . . . I could be wounded in the head, in the groin, in the stomach, in the eyes. I don't want to be wounded, crippled, or killed. What the hell am I doing here? . . . [T]he fear in me was so great, it overwhelmed my anti-fascist feelings. I had to desert. I had made the decision. I was getting out." He stayed until the end of the war.

Bessie offers a glimpse of Fisher's work as a runner during the awful last days of the Ebro offensive: "For six hours, no word from the battalion, no connection, and then, coming through the fire there are two men [runners], one of them bent with the weight of a spool of wire on his back, reeling it out across the bare *baranco* [gulley]. Orders. . . . That is [Milt] Wolff's voice speaking. . . ."

My father would have pointed to Franco, who retained power in Spain for thirty-nine years after the war. He would have said, "That's how stupid that Abraham Lincoln Brigade was. They sure backed the wrong guy." The Vets have lived with that disappointment, but they did not succumb to it. Many of them never stopped organizing and demonstrating against Franco, and they were among the first to step onto Spanish soil again when he died. Sam Gonchak, eyes shining with tears, confided to Montell, "When I arrived, I got down and kissed the earth."

Finally, it's two writers who answer the question of "why?" best for me. In 1939, Bessie wrote in *Men in Battle*:

> Men went [to Spain] . . . for various reasons but behind almost every man I met there was a common restlessness, a loneliness. In action these men would fight like devils, with the desperation of an ironbound conscience; in private conversation there was something else again. I knew, about myself, that the historical event of Spain had coincided with a long-felt compulsion to complete the destruction of the training I had received all through my youth. . . . It was necessary for me . . . to work . . . in a large body of men; to submerge myself in that mass, seeking neither distinction nor preferment . . . the opposite of a long middle-class training.

After a depressing reentry to the States in 1939, the poet Edwin Rolfe wrote, "Just what it was that sent each single one of these Americans across the Atlantic to fight for the independence of Spain will never be completely known. The bridge between the impulse and the act is a highly personal process. . . . There is a no-man's land between conviction and action into which the great majority of humankind never venture."

7

GUESSWORK

WHAT MADE DAVE leave? No one expected such behavior from him. On all sides, I hear that he was a procrastinator, a Hamlet, not someone who acted. He wrote to his parents from Spain, "I was thinking about going for over a year. I analyzed and argued with myself for quite a while. I thought of the terrible personal consequences of getting wounded and what would happen to me and to everyone I care about. I spent many hours and nights reflecting on what to do and only then did I decide to go."

But what could Dave have comprehended about the "consequences of getting wounded" or dying—the word he didn't dare enunciate—for his parents? What could he have possibly understood about such wounds and the implacable hollowness they left? Watching men die around him was horrifying, but it wasn't seeing his mother's face when she heard that she would never see him again. Or had he unconsciously inherited his parents' traumatic loss of three of their children, one from suffocation and two from smallpox? Had their anguish and their management of it become his own? Psychologists still don't know how traumas are passed on from one generation to the next, how they take up residence in our hearts and stalk us.

In any case, his mother turned around one day, and he was gone.

My mother says, "Dave went to Spain to get away from his mother. She was domineering. She pushed his father around, it bothered him." She agreed with my father on that subject. It may have been projection on both their parts. I lived with my grandparents for years, and I didn't find my grandmother overbearing. No doubt, grandchildren see things differently. My grandma Anna and Trudy were both stubborn women, and the daughter-in-law assumed her designated place around the older woman. My mother, for all her conversational bravado, was compliant. She held her tongue and resented it. She might have construed as overbearing the simple equality between Anna and Max, my grandpa, or that my grandma spoke her mind, something my mother couldn't do with my father. He forbade it, and we all obeyed that rule.

I didn't think my mother was capable of seeing how perfectly suited my grandparents were to one another. But then, on the last day of her life, when her thoughts and heart became so clear to her and she spoke in a meticulously precise vocabulary that I had never heard her use before, I realized that she did understand. I was trying to console her, or more likely myself, and knowing how much she loved my Grandpa, I said something stupid like, "You'll be seeing him soon, Mom." As if speaking to herself, she whispered "They spoke the same language, those two."

Still, what worked well between a man and a woman, a husband and wife, in no way determined the tone between a mother and her sons. Grandma was outspoken and smart and could be suspicious and manipulative. She was also possessive, preternaturally sensitive, for example, to other women's interest in my grandfather. Out of the depths of her house, she would materialize, her apron flying, hair disheveled, to remind the world—and especially another woman—of her existence.

She wasn't what you would call a tender person. Her eldest son, Phil, said, "She was an aggressive, even a scheming woman, but not coarse. You never heard a vulgar word from her. And I know she loved my father, that's probably why she never defended me in front of him. They were devoted to each other. Once in a while, when I was awake in my bed at night, I could hear them in the other room, giggling and laughing. They were never upset or sore against each other."

Until they bought their rooming house in Hurleyville, fifteen years after they arrived in America, my shrewd and resourceful grandmother had no place to put her energy. She was at loose ends. She sold tins of sardines, imported from Latvia, I'm told. She also bought and sold old clothes, lugging large shopping bags full of them into courtyards in the Bronx and barking her sales pitch up to drawn shades and blank window panes. She did what immigrants do, which is almost anything they can to earn money.

Phil and Louis didn't like spending time with her. Although they hugged and kissed their father, there was no physical affection between mother and sons. When they visited her and Max in Hurleyville after Dave was gone, my father told me, they barely set foot in the door when they were on their way out again. There wasn't much sitting around and gossiping in the Lifshitz house. Grandma's face clamped down on itself as they left, but Grandpa would smile at them and say, "Go, go. Have a good time, my sons."

In the evening, the brothers drove to a nearby hotel, snuck into the casino, danced for a couple of hours, caught a variety act. In the afternoon, they might wander down to the center of Hurleyville—all six two-story buildings—and stop in at Bochman's candy store, their summer shirts crisply ironed by my mother or grandmother, their trousers pleated in front and held in place by narrow leather belts with surprising elegant metal buckles. Sometimes they'd linger at the counter, visit with the owner-pharmacist, pick up the mail next door, then find their way back up the road again. Other times, chilled fluted glasses of chocolate egg cream, or some long-legged girls sipping their sodas on the stools next to them, slowed them down at Bochman's.

These doubly citified young men, natives of Riga and New York, were amused by the wall of inset burnished bronze mailboxes next door at the post office, each with its ridged knob, which had to be turned this way and that until the little glass door sprung open. They pulled out letters, newspapers, movie schedules, and A&P flyers.

Anna might well have become overly involved in her youngest son's life, fretting that he was too absorbed in his meetings and demonstrations and classes, that he was too serious and didn't socialize enough. She might have known that he'd spent part of a summer at a military training camp. And she couldn't but notice that he didn't have a paying job. She would have brooded over him, appreciating his political work but concerned about how he would support a family.

Dave could have felt both longing and irritation toward her, covetous of the fond glances, the loving hand on the cheek, but annoyed by the asked- and unasked-for familiarity. What will you do with your life, boychik? What are your goals? And where are your girlfriends, a handsome boy like you? He might have said, I don't know, Mama, I just don't know. Maybe he didn't answer at all. I always felt that my father wouldn't tolerate such invasions, but maybe I'm wrong. Maybe Louis longed to have someone call his bluff and, in particular, to elicit his mother's interest and attention.

Grandma and Dave came to the United States together in 1927, following Grandpa's arrival in 1925 and Louis and Phil's in 1926. Grandma packed their bags, made arrangements. When she left Latvia, she said good-bye to her mother, whom she would bring to America in the early 1930s, and her brothers, whom she never saw again. Two were killed by Stalin; one stayed in Riga and somehow survived the Nazi roundups. My grandma once recalled that on the ship to the States, she strolled on deck, struggling to keep her veil in place, to keep her hair from trailing in the breezes. If her features were pointy, a touch forbidding, her demeanor was intelligent and concentrated, and one knew she would be worth the effort to know. People noticed her, curious about why she was alone. I'll bet she enjoyed that.

Perhaps Dave wandered the boat too, looking younger than his twelve years, his limbs slightly out of control the way an adolescent's can be. Some girls giggled, eyeing him shyly. Maybe he didn't notice. He might have gone below deck to explore the engine rooms. His friend Evelyn said, "He wanted to be a worker. We all did. We were so anti-intellectual in those days."

In Riga, Dave's father had a fabulous workroom below the family's grocery shop, filled with gadgets and tools and warm lights. On the walls, dating from Max's tinsmithing days, hung a straightedge, different types of calipers, a trisquare, a tape measure, ball-peen hammers, metal shears, saws, vises, and pliers. The littlest son might sit there on a quiet Sunday, hammering and clanking next to his papa. When Dave was in America, he did an academic degree at George Washington High School, but he also took a certificate in advanced metal work. He seems to have kept his father with him.

During Dave's childhood, he was either in the company of boys and men or one woman. Indeed, it was with his mother that Dave first saw the New York skyline, his mother's clear blue eyes emptied of their usual distrust. Perhaps he noticed how lovely she was. Maybe she held his hand tightly as the island came into view, and they were astonished.

Youngest children of families of four or more siblings, especially when the youngest is a boy, can grow into confident, generous people. They are often the most beloved of children. Dave could have been such a boy. Phil was a good student, handily winning scholarships. Louis, with his alluring ways, was immensely attractive to men and women alike. Dave might have worried about what was special about himself. Still, normally when people are as nice as Dave was said to be, it's because they are easy with themselves, they have been well loved. Louis danced nimbly along his favorite byways, seductive and angry by turns, dipping in, twirling about, darting away always with a pretty girl on his arm. Phil, the doctor, the Phi Beta Kappa, grumbled, sneered, laughed derisively at the world. Dave, the fair-haired Benjamin, yielded to others, but with determined, measured steps, he went his own way.

My father said that when he told Grandma and Grandpa that Dave was dead, his mother said nothing and walked out of the room. During the following weeks, Grandpa brought food to her in their bedroom. No one saw her but him. She scarcely ate. The sons didn't know what the parents spoke about, or if they spoke. Grandpa knew she wanted to go away and never come back, that she didn't want to go on without this son. My mother told me that after Dave's death, the family thought Grandma would kill herself. Four of her sons dead. Three little boys gone a long time ago, and now, this one, the *yingele*, the baby, but almost a man. Her body recoiled, she couldn't swallow, she wouldn't walk. She held on to Max.

Hadn't she known that Dave was going to Spain? Didn't she let him go? She might have even been proud of him, her boychik, her dear boy, now more like the biblical David, showing those older brothers of his what he was capable of. The courage of the shy and the reticent. Duddy's Communism had come right up out of her body and her brothers' commitments. Maybe he didn't have the sexy charm of her *meshuggeneh* Louis or the brains of shrewd and calculating Phil, but he had something. She might well have admired the compassion and bravery of this dearest of her children.

Often we think that when the people we love let us walk away, it's because they don't care enough to hold on to us. And often, that's true. But not always. They can also let us go because they are right there with us, tasting the urgency of our desire to live, and they silently call out, Jump, jump, soar my child.

Bob Schrank told me the following story about my grandmother. She was passing along Prospect Avenue in the spring of 1939 and had reached the corner where the Communists had their soapbox. A fiery young speaker caught her attention. He was haranguing pass-ersby: "Give something—pennies, a dime, a quarter—to the refugees of the Spanish Civil War." Grandma's feet went leaden, stuck in the sidewalk like one of those giant striding Giacometti figures frozen midstep. People swayed in her direction, pulled as if by a magnet, so monstrous was the energy pushing out of her. No one was surprised when roaring out of her body came the words, "Murderer! Mur-derer! You murdered my son!" The rigidity in her limbs melted as she lunged through the crowd toward the speaker and, reaching with her bare hands for the young man, shrieked at him, "You killer!" The youngster, high on his own rhetoric and the admiration of the crowd, was horrified as her fingers sank into him. A young woman gently pried my grandma away from the street orator, who, it turns out, was Bob Schrank. Someone pulled him from the other direction. Another whispered, "That's Dave Lipton's mother."

Only once did my grandma say a word about Dave to me. It might have been that day we sat bundled up in the winter sunshine together, when I was four. She turned to me and said, "Once I had a little boy, beautiful like you. He was very dear to me."

The three sons—Louis, Phil, and Dave—the parents, and the new daughter-in-law (my mother) lived together in the Bronx. Watching Louis bully his gregarious, sensual wife probably made Dave uncom-fortable. He might have been busy with his political activities, but he was home enough to observe his brother's behavior. Louis continued to go out alone at night. He went to Miami and Cuba with his friends. Trudy stayed in the apartment with his parents. My mother told me, "I wanted to be a modern woman and not be possessive. I never tried to hold your father back." Dave said, Leave him. He was the only one. Mom's mother said, "You made your bed, now you have to sleep in it," heartbreaking advice from an earnest but unedu-cated woman who herself lived with an uncouth and violent man.

My mother tolerated anything from my father. When Louis, enraged by something she said or did, went after her, he might at times have caught his younger brother's eye; with an audience, Louis would be even more propelled by his threatened self-esteem, injured at the real or suspected slight from his young wife. He might have flown even further into his rage, certain of his brother's, any man's, approval. *Dave* would see that Louis didn't take crap from a woman! But the younger brother would certainly have been shamed by this behavior and heartsick that he couldn't stop it. "Dave told me," my mother said, "'if you stay with him, always remain independent, never dependent.'" She repeated this often, as if in its repetition, she would remember something important she had forgotten, and perhaps she could redo things, get them right this time. Then maybe my father would still love her. Or, retrospectively, perhaps she might have found the courage to leave him.

Phil remembers Louis's furies from childhood. When Louis was around nine, their parents asked him to do something he didn't want to. Phil said that Louis hurled himself on the ground, banging his head repeatedly and violently against the floor, screaming, "*Ich wille nicht, Ich wille nicht!*"—I don't want to. His parents had no idea where this rage came from. At five, he had been a compliant, good boy, the boy Grandma sent out onto the streets of Riga to peddle prized commodities during the war. They'd been proud of him. Now, they shook their heads and let him be. "That fat toad," Phil spit out, at ninety-one years old still wildly jealous of Louis. "He got away with everything, but not me, I didn't." He must have been thinking of someone else. My father, to my knowledge, had never been fat.

People didn't push my father. It wouldn't have been possible for Dave to stand up to him, tell him to treat his wife with more respect. I never saw my father control himself for his parents' benefit either, although I did notice that when my father raged at my mother, my grandpa's face would twist into a grimace, as my grandmother looked on unfazed. I heard that when my mother was pregnant with me, my father wouldn't walk in the street next to her. He said he didn't want to be seen with such an ungainly woman. It was Grandpa's arm my mother took. I remember scenes in the Bronx with my mother racing from the kitchen, locking herself in the bathroom, my father a few steps behind her.

Louis flared up fast, and his explosiveness grew more and more unpredictable. Dave would have winced at this volatility. One minute you were Louis's best friend, the next his enemy. And you never knew why. Louis might have made Dave's heart shudder, not just because Louis could casually turn away from his last victim toward someone nearby, his smile back in place, his sensitivity too, but because anger refreshed my father. That was the blood-curdling part: he thrived on anger. But you could also have such a good time with him. He got you laughing, and he laughed right along with you, tears rolling down his cheeks. Once, he was stopped for speeding three times on the same day, and the third time, he threw the keys at the cop and said, "Here, you take the damn car!"

You wanted to make my father happy, keep him amused. He was good at getting you to reveal your secrets too. He listened carefully and remembered. Later, he would remind you of what you said. Empathy would rise up out of him, warm and eager. It disarmed you. My God, you felt, what a great guy. You wanted to wander off with him for the rest of your life.

He electrified Hurleyville when he visited us in the summer. Without him, we were in paradise, as in the top strata of the tympanum above the giant door of a medieval cathedral, pleasing and harmonious but a trifle dull. No ecstasy there. When Louis arrived, the majestic pines and soft grasses, the tender flowers and nestling bushes erupted, like the flailing, doomed souls on a lower level of that same tympanum, conniving for their lives just as they are about to slip into the maw of hell. You didn't know you were gasping for air. You just knew you were alive. That is, until you weren't.

Dave knew this about Louis, the beguiling gestures and tempting smiles, the conjuring of inchoate thrills tripping off his fingertips. He lured you into his orbit. People wanted to be around him. Dave, by contrast, was a boy full of longing and good intentions. You trusted him—everyone said so—but there probably wasn't much fun in it. Hard to imagine him telling a joke. It was Schrank who said that whenever he saw Dave, he wanted to say, "What can I do for you? What can I do for you, Dave?" It's not a question he would have asked my father. But Dave was still a boy. His personality hadn't hardened into, in Phil's case, a congealed drive toward professional success or, in Louis's, the need to seduce.

When Louis wasn't grabbing people's attention, he collapsed into himself. He had no gift for friendship. But when the merest admiring look came his way, he filled up like a Thanksgiving Day balloon. Dave, on the other hand, loved the company of friends—at meetings, in study groups, organizing demonstrations, relaxing at the Red Bagel. He wasn't a loner; he needed company, to be distinguished from needing an audience.

By most people's reports, Louis sparkled and Dave glowed. Perhaps their mother kept saying to Dave, Have fun, don't be so serious. Maybe he didn't feel like smiling all the time. He saw the big shots, the guys like Schrank, and sure, he probably envied them some, but that wasn't him. Dave dressed neatly and went out into the world to do his duty. While the family might joke and argue around the dinner table, Dave would excuse himself and leave for a meeting. But at least a few photographs showed how much fun he could have.

Both Louis and Dave were readers. Dave liked American literature, poetry, and theater; Louis preferred his stories in Russian and Yiddish. Dave joined the drama club in high school and went to free concerts at the Metropolitan Museum. The culture of the New World became Dave more than it did Louis. He was younger, more supple and impressionable. His English was probably better. Anglo-Saxon culture nudged

him toward the unfamiliar, where he might muse and dally. In him and many of his generation, art flowed effortlessly, along with European Marxism. The boy molted into his own version of an American.

Maybe Dave, like Louis, walked the streets of New York whistling, marveling at the skyscrapers, the powerful upsurge of steel and concrete, the haughty stepped shoulders and curves, the fierce pride of it, these edifices afloat upon the island he saw that first day with his mother. The young Marxist might have revisited that scene, this time from the island itself. At the East Side piers, he might have gazed up at the soaring towers and felt, admiring the heights, what one feels when glimpsing a mountain from afar and then having it keep you company at its great distance, as you sip your morning coffee or explore the ramparts of a European city. Wondrous things can happen as you cross the spaces between you and the faraway, you and the gleaming American towers. Walking beneath the El on the Lower East Side at Second Avenue and Division Street, he might have smiled at the sun cutting through the train tracks overhead, splashing the sidewalk.

It is odd to me that when Dave left for Spain, he was still a virgin. He was only twenty-two, but the Communist Party encouraged sexual freedom, and he lived in a home where at least one of the men had women on his mind all the time. Dave was more like his father, though, than Louis. He was loyal, sweet tempered, feminine, some would say. Evelyn might have said so, nearly did, really. I have photos of Dave with men and women, but certainly the most tender and relaxed are those small photo-booth pictures with his male friend. Of course, Dave had many brothers; he had lived among men all his life and was comfortable with them. Even so, it's not much of a stretch to imagine Dave and his friend as sexually involved. I suggest this possibility to my father, who laughs it off. "He had plenty of girlfriends," he says. Yet when I press him, asking for details, he says he can't remember any particulars. Finally, he says, "Well, he could have been gay. I don't know."

No doubt it's a coincidence, but one of the men who spoke at Dave's memorial meeting, David McKelvey White, was gay. In *The Odyssey of the Abraham Lincoln Brigade*, Peter Carroll describes White's life and the pressure the party put on him. It "raised questions," according to Carroll, "about his lifestyle, summoning him for discussions. One day in the summer of 1945 White did not come to work at the VALB office. A colleague found him dead," a suicide.

In early April 1938, Dave applies for his first American passport. Just six months ago, in November, he became a citizen, with the name David Raphael Lipton. After his passport arrives, he makes an appointment to see a doctor for a general physical exam. Two have been recommended to him, one on East 163rd Street, the other on Central Park West. He scribbles down the possible phrasing of the note they should write on his behalf—one of the pieces of paper I found in my father's shoebox. Dave will need such a note if he decides to come up before a committee considering final applications to go to Spain. The note is worded, "This is to certify that I have this day examined Lipton, c/o Zykofsky, 816 E. 179th Street and found him in good health." He gave a friend's address to the doctor.

On the other side of the paper, Dave wrote, "The Interviewing Committee 189 2nd Ave, 2nd floor, Bill Browder."

He presents himself for an interview, his second. During the first, a year earlier, the group had asked him pointed personal and political questions and described the difficulties he and his family would face. They told him to think it over. He has. Now he is just on the other side of a decision. Obviously I don't know what made him cross over, but I have a couple of thoughts.

By the spring of 1938, momentum had built in Dave's political acts and words. This might have brought him to a place of no exit. He wasn't just thinking about Spain, he was talking about it all the time. As so many of his comrades who left to fight later declared, it was time to stop talking and time to act. I think Dave had no place to turn. He had to go to Spain. He might have been ashamed now not to go. There is a strong drive, even an instinct, in the Lifshitz/Lipton family to finish things we start, large or small, whether, as in Louis's case, that meant closing on a sale or, in Phil's, completing medical training. Dabbling wasn't a choice.

Dave's decisive step may have been easy. Maybe he had a casual encounter with someone he hadn't seen in a long while, someone from high school, and the guy said to him, "So what are you up to now, Dave? Going to City College?" And before he knew it, Dave might have said, "Actually, I'm going to Spain, you know, to fight the Fascists." And that might have been that.

After a few days, he tells his parents that he's sick of not having a paying job, and he's going to the Catskills to work in a hotel. They think that's a good idea. The only thing left for him to do is write several letters "from the Catskills" and give them to a friend who is actually going up there to work. The friend starts mailing them to Max and Anna in early June.

REUNION

ON THE MORNING of October 29, 1938, Spaniards fill the streets of Barcelona. They've come to say good-bye to the International Brigades. Dolores Ibarruri, a leader known as La Pasionaria, addresses the crowds:

> They gave up everything, their loves, their countries, home and fortune; fathers, mothers, wives, brothers, sisters and children, and they came and told us: "We are here. Your cause, Spain's cause is ours. . . . You can go proudly [now]. . . . You are history. You are legend. . . . We shall not forget you, and when the olive tree of peace puts forth its leaves again, entwined with the laurels of the Spanish Republic's victory—come back! . . . Come back to us. . . . [T]he whole Spanish people . . . will cry out with all their hearts: Long live the heroes of the International Brigades!

The Brigadistas file past her, ankle deep in flowers. Many weep. In the next days and weeks, they will go home if that's possible. Germans and Italians will go where they can. In Spain, Republicans will fight on alone for another five months, but they are no match for Franco, Hitler, and Mussolini combined. The destruction of Republican Spain is the first sign of where Europe is heading.

Franco takes Barcelona in January 1939 and Madrid by the end of March. The war officially ends on April 1, 1939. Hitler divided Czechoslovakia in September 1938. Kristallnacht took place on November 9 and 10 of the same year. The Nazis will annex Poland in September 1939. Fascism is tearing across Europe.

In early November 1996, on the occasion of a reunion marking the sixtieth anniversary of the start of the war, the surviving men and women of the International Brigades are to receive honorary Spanish citizenship in Spain, the fulfillment of Ibarruri's promise. There will also be visits to battlefields and welcoming receptions in many of the towns they defended. I have not made plans to attend. Why should I go? What would I find out about my uncle sixty years on? When Bill Wheeler asks if I'm coming, I say I can't afford it, which is also true. He's sympathetic.

Three days before the scheduled departure, eighty-six-year-old Bill drives from Athens, Georgia, to Atlanta to have lunch with a wealthy supporter of the Vets. During the meal, the millionaire asks Bill if he knows anyone who wants to go to Spain but doesn't have the money. Bill says, Well, yes I do. He walks away from the meal with all my expenses paid. When I hear what he's done, I can't say no. And now that I have this free money and am being pushed, I find that I do want to go, and I have an uncontrollable longing to call my father and say, Dad, now I'm the one going.

I do call him. He doesn't know what's gotten into me. A bunch of old guys, he says.

When the lights dim on board the plane to Madrid and people start dozing off, I find myself smiling and thinking about my uncle, my smallish uncle, his hair burnished by the sun, finding his way to the pier to catch the boat. I see him determined, looking neither left nor right.

Perhaps he's worried that he'll lose his nerve if he slows down and looks around, if he feels the sun too kindly on his neck. Maybe he'll want to change his mind and take a stroll in Central Park instead. Or maybe he feels guilty because of how excited he is to be doing this. His heart rides high in his chest. He's leaving! As he steps aboard the ship, the SS *Manhattan*, he's dazzled by its grandeur and feels proud of himself, no longer the twelve-year-old he was the last time he was on a boat, with his mother. He hands his passport to the purser, nods to the stewards, and wonders if he'll know anyone. He tries not to think of his parents, but his teeth suddenly hurt, as if they are going to fall out of his head. He grips the railing, now completely aware of what he's doing. He holds back tears. How often in his letters home he will write, "Mama, don't cry. Don't cry." But maybe he gets lucky again, and the wind shifts and the smell of the sea brings him a gift, a taste of the future. He is, after all, a fit and handsome man setting out on the adventure of his life.

The SS *Manhattan* left New York harbor for Europe on May 18, 1938. On board were six men returning to Spain for a second time. Along with Bill Wheeler were Joseph Rehil, Al Tanz, Joseph Cuban, Walter Kolowsky, and Joseph Cobert. There were also at least three new recruits: Adolph Ross (the guy from New Utrecht High School), Wilfred Mendelson, and Dave. And two stowaways: the West Coast union organizer Archie Brown and a man Brown called Ken.

Brown wrote to his wife, Hon, about the trip:

> Everybody knew where the boys [the stowaways] were going. It was funny. We were not supposed to congregate. [We] traveled from group to group. . . . The crew outdid themselves in supplying us with food. The comrades went out of their way to give us their bunks, and brought us fruit and other edibles from the dining room. . . . A group of Germans . . . kept asking the boys if they were going to Spain. Of course they got nothing out of them.

Did Dave notice the cadence of Brown's voice, his Californian inflections? That he definitely was not a New Yorker? What can I use from Brown's letter to his wife to know Dave better? Just that Dave was in proximity to this sensibility, this American—a man wanting to share his daily life with his wife as he sailed farther and farther away from her—and that Dave may have seen some of the same faces and vistas as Brown. Brown is dead now. I can't ask him if he knew Dave. When I meet Hon in Spain, I do rather want her to say that she secretly knew my uncle too.

When the ship docked in Le Havre, the men boarded a train to Paris. Brown wrote again to Hon: "As the train ran along, we came upon section gangs. We raised our fist in the air & gave them the 'Popular Front' salute. Their picks and shovel went up . . . and they excitedly returned the salute, shouting at us."

I close my eyes. The plane rocks gently over the Atlantic, and I try to see Dave in Paris. It's May, a balmy, sweet smelling time of year. I think about what the city might have looked like to him, my fair, young uncle. He knew the proportions of things in the Old World, how much smaller everything is there than in New York, the people, the buildings, the streets. Perhaps Parisian windows sweeping from floor to ceiling surprise him. Maybe New York, by comparison, seems colder now, more forbidding than this charmed and gallant city, with its gray-beige stone apartment houses and their merrily curving wrought-iron balconies and rounded zinc roofs. New York is "new" and Paris so old. Still, it is Paris, the place of dreams and love.

Is he aware of the sociability of the town? The entire city revolves around looking—out of large windows, from balconies, on café terraces, in the streets. People look directly at each other all the time. Does he notice how Parisians say, "Hello, Madame," "Good-bye, Monsieur," "Thank you, Mademoiselle," the constant social patter of the place? And what about the way they dress? Scarves confidently draped around necks and shoulders, hats at fetching angles, jackets, shirts, and blouses slyly unbuttoned. Bodies greeting each other, nodding, stiffening, inclining, withdrawing. Coming from his home, with his parents' restrained Victorian behavior and Lou's overexcitement, what does Paris look like to him?

At ten o'clock the next morning, June 1, Dave and about twenty of his comrades meet at the Gare d'Austerlitz. They wait in groups of twos and threes for their guide to arrive. They have been told not to be conspicuous. A few linger at the station bar, sip coffee from tiny cups, bite into flaky croissants. Dave might sit on a ledge at the side of the station, watching. Does the previous night's awkwardness with the prostitute nag at him? There will be plenty of other chances, he might console himself. He can't help noticing the beautiful women passing by. He's never seen anything like this before.

Perhaps he slips into thinking about his parents, imagining them sipping their hot glasses of tea, wondering about him working up in the Catskills. Better that than knowing where he actually is. He knows his parents won't last in New York. It's not for them. They'd want him to stay with them wherever they go. He's their baby, and he's not married, he doesn't have his own life. His mother is very sharp in political discussions, the sharpest in the family, really. His father keeps a certain distance, as he does with everything and everyone. Dave knows he's like that too.

Bill is a nice guy, but they're not really close. No one knows Dave well. Not Quincy, Bob, Evelyn. But they like him, he knows that. They trust him. That seems to be where it ends with everyone.

He loves his father. Pop understands. His eyes well up. He looks down at his shoes. It's not the same with his mother. Or his brothers. New York has made her harder, them too. Still, she takes him in, she sees. Does she know that marriage and children don't really interest him? That he can see teaching children, but not having them?

There's something about Dave's tight lips that might be seen as off-putting, as if he won't let you in, he'll hold back. But an astute, interested person would see through this defensiveness to a young man's diffidence. He lights a cigarette, inhales. Women pass and glance at him. He looks foreign—his serious, unflirtatious demeanor, his tight, dark-blond hair. He's not French. They think northern European, then, maybe, American. It would surprise him to know that he has something American about him, a certain confidence and distance mixed in with his eastern European Jewish melancholy. He wants to look like a worker, but he looks more like a student, an American student.

On the first evening of the reunion in Madrid, the hotel lobby vibrates with anticipation, a sea of men and women in their eighties and nineties with their children and grandchildren and friends. I'm standing on a balcony looking down on them. They are old people searching out old comrades—no insulating social vanity, no pretending not to look. They've come here from Bosnia, Russia, Cuba, Mexico, France, Britain, Holland. They are small and modest men and some women, the latter perhaps more outspoken and colorfully dressed than the men, maybe making up for their habitual neglect by historians. There are bigger, hardier men too. And still others who are tall and lean. Eyes shine, some playfully, others with amazement, some shyly. What are they remembering as they look for and find each other? Pieces of their old selves they've peeked at over the years, embellished, or shied away from?

They retain their wonder and gratitude for those days, at least at the moment, in this company. Words from *The Good Fight* reverberate in my head. Abe Osheroff musing, "Spain was the great first love of our lives"; Salaria Kee, nostalgic: "It was like a close-knit family . . . [you knew that if you were in trouble,] someone was going to find you"; Tom Page, another African American, stunned: "It was the first time I was treated like a human being. I hated to leave that country."

It's a happy gathering. Even the meager among them shed their crankiness, swelling in the moment to join this historic crowd, which perhaps, in these few moments and some others, indeed embodies the clichés one uses for such occasions. They forget their differences, their personal and political grudges. Now they are one, recalling their fight for Spain against Fascism. They fought the Good Fight. I look at them, amazed and envious.

I stay up on the balcony for a long time thinking about Dave. Who he would be here, what his feelings would be today, whom he would talk to. And then . . . I think I see him, slight of build, his hair turned white but still thick and wavy. He stands straight, like my friend, the equally petite Harry Fisher. He walks arm in arm with his wife. People greet him warmly, "Dave. For Christ's sake, it's Dave Lipton." He nods, bides his time, but mingles gladly. He's reserved yet confident. Again he reminds me of Harry, the man who wrote to his family in November 1937, "What shook me up was the effect of the bombing on the women and children. As soon as the bombs began falling, [they] began crying and yelling and ran about aimlessly. . . . When the sound of the bombs hissing downwards came, the boy [Harry was holding] lost all control of his nerves and shook like a leaf in a gale."

This Dave I'm looking at was a schoolteacher. He and his wife didn't have children. They are close, easy with each other. They have loved and trusted each other for decades. He's smiling. He tosses his head and laughs, even slaps his thigh. I never would have expected it. Something's eased up in him. A long life, I guess. And love. Obviously, I can't say whether or how long he remained a Communist, but he seems to mingle less with the guys who work in the New York office, many of them longtime party members, than with others. Maybe he left the party in 1939, when Stalin made his pact with Hitler. That's what I would have done. Or perhaps he waited until 1956, when Khrushchev disclosed Stalin's ghoulish crimes against his own people.

Of course he's here. I wouldn't have it any other way.

The evening's activities have been organized by the young Spanish Friends of the International Brigades. There are many doctors among them who, like the rest, have volunteered to help out for the week. After a few hours, we are all ushered toward a nearby arena, the Palacio de Deportes, for a concert. I try not to think that the arena's name seems to include the word "deported." I'm wishing I knew some Spanish. I want to ask somebody to explain this word to me, but I'm embarrassed. There must be something I'm missing, some pointed inversion of meaning that's important for the occasion. Still, they could have left well enough alone. I look around nervously, trying to see if anyone else is disturbed, but I spot no one. The crowd is expectant. It's 8:30 p.m. I'm happy to be with my new friends, especially Bill. We're curious about where it is, exactly, that we're going. The old people are more relaxed than I am.

Gradually, I become aware of a peculiar sound in the streets, like the clatter of hooves on cobblestones, or seashells tinkling like castanets. But there are no cobblestones or horses, and no shells. Then I understand. The city is clapping. Thousands and thousands of hands across many streets and avenues are making magical night music for the men and women of the International Brigades, they who came forty thousand strong sixty years ago. Now those who are left flow gently in their great age along the streets of Madrid, their eyes widening with disbelief as the Spanish old and young and middle aged clap and weep. As we pass before them into the arena, the crowds, as if with a single mind, part to make way, stretching out their hands, *gracias, gracias*, they cry out. Sixty years have passed, and it doesn't matter.

I try to imagine my father here. Maybe his pride in his brother would break through his derision, and he would be moved. Perhaps he'd bend his head and shed some quiet tears of his own, "My dear brother, my darling brother David, this is for you. Hear this, my brother, they love you, they are grateful and their children are grateful. They remember. Oh, Dave, why did you go? Why didn't you listen to us? We told you not to go. We told you to study. Send money, we said, it's not your fight. But no, you had to go. You had to prove something. You knew we loved you, you were our dearest. How could you leave us?"

As the last tear drops down his nose, my father's little eyes begin to slide this way and that. He takes a better look at the people near him and thinks, That one's fat, that one's slovenly, that one cares too much what his wife thinks, that one wears clothes made of polyester. What's so special about these people? They didn't die. They made money, they forgot their idealism. What did they do with their lives that's so terrific? General Electric treated me like a king when I had my appliance store. They were always offering me trips and money, but I didn't want them. Who needs them? I could have had anything. I could have been a rich man. Plus, the women.

"Anything the matter?" Bill asks, touching my arm.

"No." I shake my head. When I'm with the Vets like this, when there's an event that has to be attended, it's easy, I'm there, present, listening. But when I have to choose between them and exploring Madrid, especially the museums, I flee, grateful that paintings are dependable old friends.

Some part of me feels that I don't belong here with these people, that it's disingenuous of me to be here. It wasn't my fight. Dave's going and dying in Spain created such anguish in my family, and so much rankles and remains unsaid. My father is holding something back. I'm loathe to explore it too deeply. I fear that behind his sadness about the loss of Dave, and beyond even his disdain, is an unforgiving rage that frightens me and somehow includes me.

I keep a journal when I'm in Spain. Perusing it back in New York, I see that I've written about paintings and old men, but not much about the Spanish Civil War or my uncle. I go to museums in Spain. I find that I am particularly drawn to images of Christ. First, in the Thyssen-Bornemisza Collection, there is Duccio's *Christ and the Samaritan Woman*. Against a gold-leaf make-believe background, Jesus sits on the lip of a well. He gestures to a woman, who balances an earthen oval jug on her head, the very picture of tranquility and safety, in another world, far from what we all know lies in the future. I stare at Diego Velázquez's *Christ on the Cross* at the Prado. Jesus's tender body doesn't seem to be in pain, even as blood trickles from his hands and feet and side. A glow lights his tottering head. But the stroke of genius, the breathtaking coup marking Velázquez's deepest empathy, is the moment of privacy he inscribes on the canvas. He paints Jesus's hair falling forward over one side of his face, like the blood streaking his body and the tears we know are coursing down his mother's cheeks. No one knows what happens behind this veil of hair. Jesus is alone there. Or he is with his God.

And whom is Dave with? Whom does he belong to? What are the narratives that tell the truest stories about this man, my uncle, my father's brother?

Diego Rodriguez de Silva y Velázquez, *Christ on the Cross*, ca. 1632.
© Madrid, Museo Nacional del Prado

My father communicated this to us: be brave and idealistic and I will love you like I did my brother. But he also said: be brave and idealistic and you will die for nothing, like Dave. Die for nothing, be a fool, and I will always have contempt for you.

When I was a girl, I read Sholem Asch's *The Nazarene*. It came along through my mother's Communist book club, I think. In it, Judas betrays Jesus because Jesus chooses him to do so. In this interpretation, were it not for Judas, Jesus would not be crucified, and the world would not be redeemed. Jesus demands betrayal as a sign of love from Judas. I have always found this to be a perverse idea. One can say that Judas loves Jesus enough to obey his master's demand. And Jesus loves Judas, and he dreads him. When has there ever been such a *chagrin d'amour*? To need and cherish someone who loves you, and to know that this same person will—and does—betray you. The horror of it—and alas its prosaicism in real life—an act destined to be beyond comprehension. Of course Judas killed himself.

I always sensed my father's potential to betray, not out of a spiritual and philosophical urgency or an existential dread, but because somewhere, revenge appealed to him, whatever the excuses. I could not know, however, the extent of this drive in him, nor could I possibly imagine just how odious it might be.

Some of the old Brigadistas are still extremely attractive physically. There's Milt Wolff, the prince of the Lincolns, the last commander of the brigade and one of the handsomest men in the world when he was young. I had corresponded with him in the United States about my uncle. He responded, Sorry, I didn't know him. But he offered some helpful suggestions. I telephoned, we talked about this and that. I kept pictures of him in Spain in front of me. Dark, dark eyes, thick, wavy brown hair, a sexy grin. He is said to have stolen a girlfriend from Hemingway.

In Madrid, I meet Milt face to face. He's still dashing, somewhat

stooped perhaps—he had been six feet three inches tall, a height hard
to believe for an immigrant boy from Brooklyn in the 1930s—with
the most beautiful head of gray hair stylishly cut, heavy brows, and
mischievous eyes. Mary Rolfe, wife of the poet and Veteran Edwin
Rolfe, described him in a letter from October 1938: "Milton Wolff,
that twenty-three year old major is a dynamo of energy. He doesn't
talk, he roars—he doesn't walk, he lopes—a genuine kid who went
up in the ranks and became a major some weeks before his twenty-
third birthday . . . when he laughs everyone laughs—it's so infectious."

Some months before the reunion, I read Wolff's novel about the
Spanish Civil War, *Another Hill.* We talk about it and about writing in
general. "You know," he says to me on the phone, "I have a friend
who tells me, 'I have a great book in me, I know it. I just can't get it
out.' But he never sits down and writes. He's a social butterfly. If
you're writing a book, that's what you have to do, day in and day out,
sit in front of the computer and write." That's an eighty-year-old
man talking, and one who was an activist all his life, not a writer. I
sense that he has just described himself. When we speak, he is still
hoping to write another book.

Milt wrote to his mother from the front about a trip to Madrid
where he found "hot baths—clean beds—gorgeous women—heavenly
wines—decent meals—friendly people—candy, cake, ices, and beer!!!
. . . and I almost forgot the American movies and American whiskey.
. . . P.S. Still your favorite son, Mom? Enclosed find five postcards."

No sooner do I meet Milt in the hotel lobby than he proposes
that I accompany him to a Hemingway dinner the following week in
New York. I'm listening. He had been friends with Hemingway. If
I'm interested, he says, I'd have to make all the arrangements—switch
his homeward-bound flight, get him a hotel room in New York, etc.
I'm taken aback and, lying, I reply that I'm not a good organizer, but
I'd be glad to go to the dinner if he finds someone else to make the
plans. He laughs. "Sure, sweetheart."

One day during the following week, I am on a bus with Milt traveling the battlefields of Belchite, Caspe, Batea, and Gandesa. Milt and a former marine who'd been in Vietnam are leading a bus tour. I don't really trust the two of them to know where they're going. The rest of us have no way to verify whether we are actually in a particular spot or not. But I give myself over to it. And some places there is no disputing. Like the town of Belchite, left in ruins by Franco to show people what he did, and that he could do it again.

Milt sits in front of me and to the right across the aisle. I watch him intently, looking for the commander of sixty years ago, the fearless boy, unusually tall, miraculously never wounded. Perhaps he knows that I'm looking at him. Women—maybe men too—have always looked at Milt. In the afternoon, I notice him half-consciously irritated by the hot sun beating down on him from the right. Distractedly, he fiddles with the window curtain. He gently flings it free of its clasp. I turn away.

Dave probably didn't know Milt personally, might not have wanted to. But Dave surely saw him. I wonder what he thought. Milt might have reminded him of Lou, as he does me. The twinkle in his eye, the simmering heat, the physical ease. They say Wolff was brave. I believe it.

As we drive through the mountains of Spain, I think of Dave in the landscape, smoking with comrades, crawling across rubble-strewn terrain, carrying a wounded friend. Bill has repeated, "Dave was a good soldier, he did what had to be done and didn't complain." Bill always ends on that, the not complaining.

By the time Dave arrived in Spain, it was illegal to cross over from France. That's why they climbed the Pyrenees by foot. I'm sure Dave found crossing the mountains more difficult than he'd anticipated. He had no experience of that kind of topography. During summers in Riga, his family had gone to the beach. They did the same in New York, to Orchard and sometimes Jones Beach. They frequented the Catskills too, but where they went weren't the actual mountains, even if that's the word people used for the gentle hills and the bundle of towns—including Liberty, Monticello, Loch Sheldrake, Hurleyville, Mountaindale, and South Fallsburg—marking the foothills of the Catskill chain. "The mountains," they said, as only city-dwellers will refer to some rolling hills that are only a bit higher than up at the Cloisters in Manhattan's Fort Tryon Park. And now he was hiking a powerful mountain range to Spain, lugging his body, which was already aching in ways he never knew it could.

Most of the men were utterly green. "You felt," wrote Alvah Bessie,

[that many of these guys] will never see their friends or families again; they don't know what they're getting into; their idealism has blinded them to the reality of what they will have to face. And you knew immediately that you were wrong; that they were so far from being blind that it might be said of them that they were among the first soldiers in the history of the world who really knew what they were about. . . . Their very presence on the French frontier was [a sign] of their understanding and their clarity; no one had made them come, no force but an inner force had brought them.

I don't know if I agree. No one can imagine his or her own death. Another volunteer, Henry Eaton, wrote home in another voice entirely, "All along the road to the burning, ruined town of Brunete we had the human qualities drained from our vitals. We became automatons, unable to feel because horror had surpassed our ability to meet it. . . . I have no emotions left to drive me crazy." Fear had numbed him. Eaton died in Brunete.

As the men crossed the Pyrenees, they were often silent. They pulled along, one behind the other. Joe Dallet, a Dartmouth graduate who had been a union organizer and steelworker before the war, wrote to his girlfriend that the mountains are magnificent, and cruel. Three of our group played out and had to be virtually carried the last half of the trip. . . . Some groups have crossed in such darkness that they couldn't see their footing at all and had to hold on to the coat of the man ahead. . . . The last peak was a 5,000-foot climb over loose and jagged rock, through thick stiff underbrush, etc. And we had to race against sunrise to get over without being seen. I carried a 165-lb guy practically by myself that whole climb.

My uncle may have stumbled at a certain point too, and at that moment, he might have thought of his mother. If he got hurt, what would happen to her? If he died. He knows people don't like her, her aloofness and seeming indifference, but she has a playful side. Dave might remember her eyes smiling at him, flirting with him. The ship to America. This boy now climbing toward Spain begins to be hungry, a gnawing feeling in his stomach, a touch of nausea. He looks up from the path for a moment, takes in the majesty of the night sky and all the men together pushing across to Spain, to fight for freedom. Yes, this is exactly what he wants to be doing. He wants this challenge. He wants to change the world. And when he finally crosses the border, he laughs and cries with the others, and they hug one another and rest. It is early June 1938.

In retrospect, we realize that what came to be known as the Great Retreats were already over by May 1938. Franco would win, brutally, unforgivingly. But in the early summer of 1938, a powerful Republican army offensive is about to start. They are going to cross the Ebro River and try to retake land the Fascists won in the spring. The group portrait of Dave sitting under a tree with about twenty other men is taken during this offensive.

When they arrive in Spain, they stay for a day in Figueres. Six months earlier, Dr. John Simon described it as the "[m]ost wonderful

place I ever saw. All languages understood—regardless of what you say, someone can understand it." They sang "all songs in a great big ancient fort . . . Red songs, German, French, Greek, Armenian, Yiddish." But when Dave and Adolph Ross arrive, Ross remembers, "The camp was run by men who were wounded, had lost limbs, their heads were wrapped in bandages. They were chopped-up guys. They looked at us newcomers with pity. They knew how hopeless the situation was. Plus, look, we were city boys. We had to adjust to the hills, the physical and emotional conditions, the military sensibilities." Jack Shafran, Harry Fisher's friend from New York, adds, "Only a trickle of volunteers were coming at this time. The war was lost. We knew it." Perhaps the new green recruits like Dave chalk up the discouraging talk to the penetration of subversives.

One day during the reunion, five hundred of us are taken to a union hall outside of Madrid. I am seated with a Vet, his daughter, and his son-in-law. The Vet had been a commissar during the war. He looks out at the world from under thick brows, his eyes steady, Picasso eyes. You can't upset him, and he never smiles. No one is precious to him. The look is meant to communicate fairness, but it's just a cold, manipulative stare that marks out territory, announces who has power and who doesn't. This man listens carefully but never takes your side out of sympathy. He has none. To his credit, he intends to do the right thing politically. His heart will never get in the way, though. It won't be a problem. He has no empathy but plenty of libido, even at eighty-three. A woman would only want him, however, if hostility and menace were her cup of tea, if she had an appetite for being criticized and the need for a man's rage and neediness, which only she could assuage in the deep of night, when nobody would know. I notice that the man's daughter, at around forty-five, is very nervous. She plays the little girl with her short curly hair, high-pitched, breathless voice, and endless questions and disbelief. My uncle's children would be different. He was, after all, a retiring man, compassionate and cautious, wily on his own time and sweet. Not a man's man.

Then there is Jacques, from Holland. I sit next to him at a banquet lunch for the Internationals in Badalona. He talks loudly and pokes me a lot with his elbow. It bothers me at first, but then I think it must be a Dutch style I'm not familiar with, like the people falling all over each other and off stools, benches, and beds in Dutch paintings by Jan Steen and David Teniers. Jacques has a repertory of rousing war stories. I comment on his joviality. He looks at me and asks, "What's the use of feeling bad?" But then he adds, no doubt to please me, that he lost his citizenship when he returned to Holland after the war. He's come to Spain alone.

"Why are you here now?" I ask.

"My children. My children thought it would be good for me."

"Were they right?"

"Oh, yes." He smiles broadly, this large-headed, blue-eyed man with his straight fair hair brushed back. "I left my wife with them. She has Alzheimer's now." His face goes flaccid. I rest my hand on his arm. He looks down and sighs, "The hardest part is not having her next to me in the bed anymore."

So here are these guys in their eighties and nineties, old men with desire. They will not and would not be victims. And it would have been so very easy. They lost in Spain. As Albert Camus so cannily wrote, the war taught them "that one can be right and yet be vanquished, that force can subdue the spirit, that there are times when courage does not have its reward." Yet so many of them never gave up.

With Milt and his ex-marine pal, I retrace the Battle of the Ebro. My uncle was shot at the end of this offensive on Hill 666, near the town of Gandesa. He described the battle in separate letters to his parents and brother. To Lou he wrote, very briefly and in English, on August 10: "Just returned from that wonderful offensive you must have read about. Saw plenty of action and am writing to let you know I am fine and whole. Well, what do you think of Loyalist Spain now—What a victory. No more time. Have not heard from the States yet. How is everything?" And to his parents, a day earlier, in Yiddish: "I only hope you have received my first letter. . . .You probably have read about our victory in Spain, the offensive we made and how we pushed the fascists back. Everyone feels it is a decisive victory." He asked several questions about the family and ended the letter, "Well, beloved family . . . all of you be healthy and don't worry about me. Mother, don't cry." It's odd that he sent a separate letter to Lou just a day afterward, as the letter to his parents included Louis, Phil, and my mother.

The offensive starts near midnight on July 24, 1938. There is tremendous confidence among the International Brigades. This could change everything. Milt Wolff, commander of the battalion, prepares his men with these words:

> At any moment now we are going to cross the Ebro. . . . Over eighty thousand men will be crossing simultaneously. . . . We are going to relieve the pressure on Valencia. We are going to . . . penetrate deep into Fascist territory. . . . Behind us will come trucks and ambulances, with munitions, food and supplies. . . . This action has been planned long in advance, and we have plenty of information from our sources behind the Fascist lines. The forces facing us . . . are largely new recruits, youngsters who have seen no action. . . . We know where their troops are located and exactly how many there are. We know where to find their ammunition dumps. . . . The main line of fortifications we will meet when we come to it . . . at Gandesa, which our American comrades may remember. We are going to avenge our comrades who fell there last April. . . . Every man is to stand by, prepared to move at a moment's notice. *Viva la República!*

This is Wolff at twenty-three! Yet I also remember the jaded words of a brigade officer, General Golz, in Hemingway's *For Whom the Bell Tolls*. He says to the young American explosives expert Robert Jordan, "What is to guarantee that my orders are not changed? . . . What is to guarantee that it starts within six hours of when it should start? Has *any* attack ever been as it should?"

The order comes, and the Internationals cross early on July 25. They quickly take the town of Fatarella. On July 28, the Lincolns are in a battle at Villalba de los Arcos, just north of the town of Gandesa. Does Dave, like his comrade Ben Gardner, an artist, enjoy "the wonderful feeling of holding a rifle with bayonet, guarding Democracy"? Does he identify with Dave Gordon's words to his wife? "There is a terrible beauty in watching a dog-fight. Planes screaming, spitting heavy machine-gun bullets at each other, weaving, diving, soaring, chasing, turning over and over backwards, forwards and sideways." Could Dave express this excitement and pleasure to his parents, in the face of not hearing from them, not knowing whether they have forgiven him? Mightn't such declarations be like relishing moments with a new lover and describing them to the lover you've just left? Dave never writes about the complicated and contradictory satisfactions of his incredible journey. His letters are practical, dutiful, casually informative.

Archie Brown describes Hill 666, one of the final sites of the Battle of the Ebro: "All the terrain was steep and rough. Morning showed a scene of a blackened, war-torn, and destroyed land. Dead burros lay everywhere. Bodies were everywhere too. They stank." Bessie remembers:

> For two and a half hours we bent to the forty-degree angle, twisting and turning, slipping and stumbling up the almost impassable way. There was one thought in our minds: it's going to be hell getting food, water and munitions up this hill; it's going to be tough for the wounded. . . . God never made a more desolate stretch of territory. . . . It looked like a landscape on the moon—tumbled, crumbling rock, black and slippery; burnt-off shrubbery that caught our trouser legs and tripped us up. We slipped and fell, stumbled and cursed. . . . Even before dawn it was possible to see that there was no cover here; there were no trees . . . no bushes . . . the earth itself was stone. . . . And there were no fortifications facing the enemy. . . . All day, hour after hour they kept it up. They covered our parapets and every inch of the back side of the hill. They wanted, by the sheer weight of their steel, to blow us off that hill.

Up there on 666, every day they hear the rumors of withdrawal, that they are all going home soon.

Only four hundred of the seven hundred men in the battalion are now active. In early August, they are pounded by artillery in what becomes known as the Valley of Death. The historian Hugh Thomas writes, "All day and every day the nationalist aeroplanes, sometimes two hundred at the same time, circled over the republican lines. . . . [They] dropped an average of 10,000 pounds of bombs every day."

In between the shelling, Dave, like his comrades, probably lights a cigarette, savoring the inhale, the rush, the coy skeins of smoke floating skyward. He wishes Lou could see him, a grown-up fighting for Spain, fighting for all the oppressed in Spain, in the United States, everywhere. Maybe he wishes that the young man in the small photo-booth pictures could see him too. And Bob Schrank. In mid-August, he writes to Lou and his parents again. He's so ashamed of the lies he told. He's never lied to them before. Louis is the liar, not him, he thinks. How did Louis find him? He's clever. He could have gone over to the YCL club, chatted with some of the guys, and found out that way. But what a nasty letter he'd sent. He had called Dave selfish and indifferent to his parents, putting a cause above the family.

Then there is that last letter that Bill thought was to my father. He gives it to Bill. Then he takes it back. What was in it?

Maybe Dave is glad to be far from his family and New York. Here, he knows what the stakes are. What it feels like on the edge of death, the edge of life, flying on the tattered wings of dwindling hope but also sagging into despair. The unbearable, unavoidable longing it all brings. He is sensate in ways unfamiliar. Until the sniper gets Dave, he may never have felt as whole before, absorbed in this world of fear and ecstasy and unreflective action, following orders and his body's instinct to survive, all in the interest of saving people from their appalling destinies as he reaches for his own.

Long-forgotten memories disturb him. The dead and wounded collapse, moaning around him. He thinks of his brother Louis out on the streets of a devastated Riga when he was a child. What was his mother thinking? They say that when killing is all around you, it doesn't quite register. It's your own life you are trying to save first of all. I have read Holocaust accounts, Charlotte Delbo's, for example, in which the reader sits behind Delbo's eyes as she coldly watches death snuff out the woman next to her.

Did my uncle kill, watch others killed, and feel nothing? No horror, no taste of unholiness? Thou shalt not kill. Remember, thou shalt not kill. That basic respect for human life over centuries. Improve yourself for a better world. Read Talmud, study. But most of all: thou shalt not kill. Dave, who were you there in Spain, my young uncle? Why, of course, you were everyone and everything you would ever be and had been. It was all right there, wasn't it?

9

IN THE BALANCE

"WHAT I CAN'T shake," Bill says, "is that he gave me this letter and asked for it back the next day, and there was some very driving thing that made him write it in the first place and then made him tear it up."

In the earlier letter of August 9, a week before this exchange with Bill, Dave had written:

Dear Mother, Father, Leipke, Feifke and Trudy,
How is everyone in my beloved family? It has been a few weeks that have gone by since I last wrote you, and I have not written because I have no time. . . . Everything here is going well. I feel very well and I'm working very hard for the Republic. . . .

As for me, there is nothing to worry about. I am healthy and strong. The only thing that troubles me is that I know how long it takes for a letter to arrive from Spain and you are all probably worried about me. Don't worry yourselves please, and be very brave and very good anti-fascists. I have not heard from you and I wonder how all of you are feeling. Here, the weather is very cold at night and very hot during the day. . . .

Nu, how are Papa and Mama? Does he have work? . . . Now

that your son is in Spain, are you perhaps working for the cause in
Spain? What is the situation about cigarettes? Is it hot in New York?
How is Trudy's foot? There are so many things I want to know.

Well, beloved family, I don't have anything else to write. . . .
Mother, don't cry.

your son and brother,
Duddy

People say that Dave began to change in Spain. Adolph Ross
remembers him erupting at someone trying to get ahead of him in
the food line. Someone else, who knew him from the Bronx, noticed
that his attention wandered when you were talking to him, that he
was there in front of you but at the same time far away, riveted perhaps by two men in intense conversation or the smirk on the face of
the guy walking by or the smell of fresh bread floating over from the
field oven. This was not the empathic fellow they knew, unthreaten-
ing, efficient, thoughtful. Of course, he might have said the same of
them; fear, loneliness, and boredom disfigured each of them.

Dave waits for his name during mail call, listening but trying not to
at the same time. If only he'd hear from them. No one has written.
Just that first letter from Louis. Each time Dave writes home, he
means to be casual when letting his parents know that he hasn't
received any mail. His words unfold gently. But in each letter, he
repeats it.

Mail call is over. Nothing for Dave Lipton. He gets up, pulls a
newspaper from a stack nearby, checks his supply of bullets, tops up
his canteen.

On August 16, Dave hands Bill the letter, embarrassed, "In case
. . ." Bill comforts him and says, "Just keep your head and fanny
down." The next day, Dave asks for the letter back. On August 20,
he's walking toward Bill, asking him something, and he forgets the

rules. Is something stirring in the distance, the flap of a bird's wings, a harsh voice hurtling across the valley, those two men whispering to each other again? Whatever it is, Dave stands bolt upright, and the sniper zeros in on his heart.

My father told him—and, later on, me—in the only letter he sent to Spain that Dave should not send mail to his parents' home but rather to their uncle Lazar Slavin, Grandma's younger brother. Dave apparently didn't ask any questions. As the fighting grew more intense, indifference to everything except staying alive escalated. There was no reason to interrogate a single additional thing. And Louis's tone probably suggested that Dave shouldn't ask, and Dave's relationship to Lou was too complicated to revisit just then. No doubt Dave was only vaguely aware of how he was both drawn to and repelled by his brother. Maybe guilt was mixed in too, the younger brother unmasking the older brother's bravura, as Dave, the quieter one, turned out to be the warrior.

Could Dave have been losing confidence then? Did he in fact obsess over Louis's mailing instructions? Maybe Louis was protecting their parents by telling him to send his letters to Lazar. Or perhaps Louis had become more politically engaged, and this intricate choreography was his way of fighting for the Republic too, of being with his brother, and at the same time of not overwhelming their parents with worry? Or was Louis thinking that his parents would be moving again or the mailboxes in their apartment building weren't secure? There were many plausible explanations, though none of them would have provided the comfort Dave needed. We all know what not getting mail or a phone call feels like—an agony layered to infinity. Dave's condition was approaching the intolerable.

Still, he did what his brother asked. He focused on his own part, the letters—written on his lap in soft pencil, on small sheets of lined paper—composed with love, sent out across the Spanish hills and mountains and over the sea, heading west to New York. While he wrote, balancing the pad, composing the phrases, imagining his mother and father reading them, he was fine. The calm might have stretched into a day or two, or even until a few days before the next mail delivery.

Alongside grisly encounters with dying comrades in skirmishes during which the Republicans were horribly underequipped, Dave might have also gone with members of his squad to help out in the fields and share a meal with a farmer and his family. For men and women fighting in the International Brigades, a precious part of what they did in Spain was to socialize and work with the local population. The Spanish Civil War wasn't a war of abstractions for them, and the relative informality of the rules of behavior encouraged humanizing and particularizing each situation they found themselves in.

Dave's Spanish was excellent. Eating and working with a local family would have been enjoyable for him, although laboring in a field was more unknown to this city boy than holding a gun was. But where did he file the blunt existential shock of ferocious combat rubbing up against warm human contact just two hundred yards down the road? Or was that just life in Spain at that moment? Only subsequent narratives split them off from one another.

In his letter to Bob Schrank and his friends, Dave wrote, "Not one inch of fertile land is wasted and you see Spaniards working way into twilight wrestling out of stony nature—green bliss!" He was fairly humming with pride in the same letter when he wrote, "Wait until we meet and I will be willing to tell you tales right through the night." To these same friends in New York, Dave sent a taste of life around him: "cocky hats and deep-tanned faces," "cherry trees filled with ripe cherries and sticky fingers," "rickety villages and hard parched soil; stone houses and tiny, unpaved, mysterious streets."

It was not all dejection and waiting on letters. "The actual fighting with weapons is the highest stage a real communist can ask for," wrote Robert Hale Merriman, twenty-eight, in his diary in Spain. "[I'm] about to lead the first battalion of Americans in this war." Dave must have been thrilled that, for the first time in his life, he was fighting the enemy with more than words, demonstrations, and strikes.

Alvah Bessie once again captured best of all what this fight meant to these politically sophisticated and highly motivated mostly young people. Bessie loaded all his longings to be a fully sentient, responsive human being onto realizing his politics on the ground in Spain. He wrote in 1939, right after his return:

> Yes [on the battlefield], you can think of love. The love you have never had and could not give. . . . And you are afraid that you will die without that love; you are not just afraid to *die*. And this is the meaning of it all (the people's war); these men behind these fragile rocks, these men whose tender flesh is torn to pieces by the hot and ragged steel; they could not accept their death with such good grace if they did not love so deeply and so well—were not determined that love must come alive into the world. What other reason could there be for dying? What other reason for this blood upon your hands?

Dave did not write to his parents of such sentiments. He described his physical condition, told them how much he'd love to hear from them and how much he hoped they would forgive him. Then he asked them to send packages: "cigarettes are the most important . . . chicken pudding, jam or preserves, cheese (Swiss or the 3 cornered American cheese), a small can-opener and chocolate (Nestle's milk). . . ." In these modest demands, we hear a boy writing home, maybe a boy writing to his mother.

Mail call came round again. Still nothing for Dave.

There never would be any mail for Dave, and here is the simple reason why: Dave's parents never received any of his mail. Not one single letter.

Louis did pick up his brother's letters every couple of weeks from their uncle Lazar, as arranged. It was agreed that he would bring them to his parents. Initially, I'm sure, he planned to rush home with them, so his mother and father could respond immediately. But then it may have occurred to him that he would first have to explain everything, reveal that Dave was not in the Catskills but in Spain with a gun in his hand, fighting in a war. They would become irate. Grandma would groan and scream, she might start hitting her head against the wall. They would turn on him, Louis, the messenger. These thoughts would have made my father terrifically uncomfortable.

He didn't go directly home that first day, or the next, or the time after that.

Whenever Louis went to Lazar's house, he would have to explain to his aunt and uncle that he hadn't yet given his parents the letters, that the right moment hadn't presented itself. Understanding the sensitivity of the situation, they were patient, just as Harry Fisher's sister Sal was when he wrote to her on July 7, 1937, "I really don't think it is necessary to let mom know that I am in Spain yet." Louis certainly left his aunt and uncle's house with the intention of going to his parents' apartment. But something always stopped him. He told me this in great detail and evident dismay near the end of his life. A flashy movie poster drew him into an air-conditioned theater. A candy store beckoned with the promise of an ice-cold root beer and a chat with the guy behind the soda fountain. Or he just ran into a friend and fell into conversation.

Whatever happened and for whatever reason, *Louis never gave his parents Dave's letters*. Not the first ones and not the last ones. The boy's words of love and remorse never reached his mother and father. And that is why he never heard from them. Or from anyone else in his family.

What did my father think he was doing when he tucked the letters first into his pockets, then into the shoebox? Was he actually waiting for the perfect day, when his mother had just finished cleaning and the windows glistened, the floors and mirrors shone? An afternoon when a brisket stew was simmering on the stove, and Grandpa was sitting by the window reading the *Freiheit*? Surely he thought there would be such a moment, such a day, and he would pull out all the tender letters and hand them to his parents, smiling.

As the weeks and months passed, he probably fretted over the accumulating letters and the now impossibly complicated explanations he would have to give. What would he say to them? But then, knowing my father, he probably got angry. Forget about it, he might have counseled himself. It's no big deal. What was going to Spain about anyway? What was so important that this *pisher*—this baby—brother of his was doing? He, Louis, was the Man, wasn't he, the boxer, the gambler, the tough guy? Dave was just a quiet, good boy. How did he end up being the one who went to Spain anyway? It's all *narishkeit*, nonsense. My father would come back to himself a big shot, *the* Lifshitz big shot. Nobody would know anything. Letters shmetters! It would all go away.

He told no one what he had done. And of course, his parents never asked about any letters from Spain. As far as they were concerned, their son was working in a hotel in the Catskills.

And then it was too late for letters.

Early in December 1938—four months after Louis last heard from Dave—he received mail from Ben Katine conveying the news of his brother's death. Soon afterward, he met Katine at the dock where his ship had arrived from Europe. For four months, Louis had known that something was terribly wrong. Time held him by the throat as he anxiously rehearsed Dave's imminent return. Until the moment when that was no longer possible, and Louis stood in front of Dave's friend at the pier, holding the small packet of Dave's possessions that Ben had handed to him. That's the day the tears started. Louis went home and told his parents everything.

For my grandparents, there was no solace of truths already con-
fessed, couched in the love and respect that Dave had always shown
them. Nor did their boy's bravery and determination figure for them.
How could it? No thick carpet of affection and empathy cushioned
their fall. There were only the false Catskills letters and a son who
had lied to them, whom they would never see again.

My father told me that Dave once said to him, "You know, Lou, you
look like a poet." That made Louis happy. He loved the idea. People
flattered my father. It was a sort of bribery, an attempt to short-
circuit his aggression. But I don't think that's what Dave was doing. I
think Dave was aware of Louis's fantasies, of how he longed to be a
person of substance—yes, a writer—something more than a flashy
guy. And Louis's younger brother wanted to encourage him, to help
him find the confidence to stick to something and be grand. The boy
seems to have had a knack, almost a clairvoyance, for seeing what
people needed. He had told Trudy not to marry Lou and coached
Evelyn when she felt ill at ease at meetings.

Generally, my father didn't believe the nice things people said
about him. He worried that they saw through his swagger to his
longings, and this humiliated him. In fact, he loathed the people who
flattered him. But perhaps he knew that Dave wasn't doing that. Even
my father knew love when he saw it. I bet Dave was the only person
in the world who my father never thought would hurt him. Maybe
that's why he fell apart when Dave left, and why he never forgave
him for leaving. And why part of him wanted to hurt Dave.

Louis treated Dave like he did everyone. Louis was Number One.
But in this case, his egotism may have played a part in his brother's
death. It's possible that if Dave had heard from his parents, he might
have been more alert in the Sierra Pandols during that last Ebro
offensive. He might have taken fewer chances.

Dave may have heard from a comrade that someone had met his

mother in the street and started talking to her about her son in Spain—something I know took place—and that she had insisted that it wasn't her son, because he was in the Catskills. Dave would have understood then that his mother and father had never received his letters, that his mother had never learned how sorry he was to have hurt her, how very much he loved her, how much he needed to be forgiven. Could Louis have actually done this to him and their parents? He could barely believe it. Or had the mail just never arrived? None of it? In all that time?

If Louis couldn't bring Dave into focus through the haze and murmur of his self-absorption, he couldn't see anyone else either. The days when he didn't bring the letters to his parents, it wasn't because he didn't love Dave, exactly, although jealousy and vindictiveness played their parts. It was more that he had to have that soda, that movie, that conversation, that whoosh of pleasure he couldn't say no to. Perhaps he couldn't bear the thought of seeing his parents suffer. He surely persuaded himself that it wouldn't matter in the long run, that Dave would be home soon.

So Dad didn't exactly not love Dave. It was just that in the moment, he forgot, as his narcissism—and, let's be frank here, his cowardice and maybe his competitiveness too—blinded him, and he looked at life in the only mirror he ever held up to it, the mirror that showed him himself.

Louis acted out of a certain compulsion, his habitual carelessness determining his actions. He didn't mean anything by it. Look, he thought, each day brings another, no one knows what's coming next. Maybe he thought he'd find himself on an open road again, the wind riffling his hair, the sun warm on his hands and face, an Italian tenor crooning on the radio. And Dave? Well, that was over, wasn't it? Nothing to be done now.

But in our family, Dave's death never got to be over.

Meanwhile, Dave passed his last—probably chillingly lonely, sometimes exhilaratingly hopeful—weeks on Spanish soil with new friends. Soul-splintering experience did not entirely bury optimism and the pleasures of camaraderie and shared dreams. At moments, he filled up with pride and even confidence, committed to the resplendent and—we now know—doomed vision of the Internationals, to protecting the world from Fascism. It had to have been thrilling too.

At the memorial for Dave in the Bronx on January 18, 1939, Bill Wheeler, David McKelvy White, and Yale Stuart spoke. So did Dave's brother Phil. Louis was unable to speak. He couldn't stop crying.

Had Dave been there, sitting in the last row, rocking back on his chair, he might have shaken his head sadly, nodding: Poor Louis, always messing things up. I know he loved me, and now he's lost me. And he's lost the chance to move away from the family, make his own life. Guilt will bind him to them—married when he doesn't want to be, probably a parent when children hold no attraction for him. And he'll never write. That's over now. Sure, there will be moments when he makes a foray onto the dance floor, a gleam back in his eye, and he'll charge full steam ahead into what might have been. I wouldn't change places with him for anything.

Had I been there sitting off to the side behind my father and Phil, I would have noticed cool Phil pulled back behind his wayward emotions. No surprises there. But my father, my poor father, shrunken to half his size, shaking with sobs. That would have stunned me. What was it? Sorrow, desperation, shame? Had there been a real relationship with Dave, or was it all projection and fantasy? No, he loved Dave. He'd miss him, his softness and youth—his baby brother—his buoyancy and sweetness. His honesty. My father would never have a friend like that again. He wouldn't allow it, and he probably didn't deserve it.

As for me, well, sitting there, I am so proud of Dave, so very proud that he was one of us, my family. I know how much his young life gave me. Without him and his friends, people like me never would have poured out onto the streets against the war in Vietnam, ridden the buses and marched for civil rights, created the women's movement and the gay liberation movement. We drew on their courage and large desires against what was sensible, and against our parents' wills.

My mother was the exceptional parent. She reveled in the chutzpah Dave encouraged in her, the desire to stand her ground as a working person. She was, I believe, secretly thrilled to see me strike out in the same directions she had traveled as a young Communist next to Dave. She peered out from behind the bleak burden of her marriage, and she pushed me forward into my uncle's arms, where no doubt she would have so liked to be again. Wordlessly, she urged me, Go ahead, stand up for your beliefs, don't be afraid, and for God's sake, don't forget to eat!

Acknowledgments

Trudy Lipton, my mother, comes first. She kept Dave Lipton's memory alive when, every year on what seemed like a perennially beautiful spring day, she put on her best suit and set off in her determined way to join the Veterans of the Abraham Lincoln Brigade during their yearly reunion in downtown Manhattan.

So many thanks to Bill Wheeler, that kind, committed man who went to Spain twice, once after being seriously wounded in the Battle of Jarama. Despite the immense sadness of the Fascist victory in Spain, Bill, like so many of the Vets, never lost heart or faith in the rightness of what they had done.

Harry Fisher, another devoted Veteran who wouldn't let his history die, lent me books and never tired of telling me stories from his and his friends' pasts.

Abe Smorodin, a Vet who worked in the VALB office on Union Square, vaguely mocked me—why did it take you so long to get around to looking for us? But he never stinted on finding names, addresses, and telephone numbers he thought I could use.

I couldn't have written this book without the inspiration of the life of historian, poet, and memoirist Peter Carroll and his monumental study *The Odyssey of the Abraham Lincoln Brigade: Americans in the Spanish Civil War.*

My brother-in-law Stuart Aptekar, poet of the soul and fine jazz trumpet player, came up with my title.

Jean Casella, an intrepid reader and critic, was a one-person Eunice Lipton–mobilizing unit for a while.

Mieke Bal was another careful critic, editor, and booster. I also had discerning readers in Linn Underhill, Joan Rosenbaum, Lucy Aptekar, and Fraser Ottonelli.

Diane Mancher, publicity maven, stood in as agent when I needed her, and novelist Michele Zackheim gave me more than moral support on the business end of things.

Jean-Jacques Jauffret nudged me into reconsidering this book when I had quite walked away from it. It didn't hurt that Jauffret is not only a dear friend and great chef, but also a brilliant filmmaker.

Arnaud Meunier's generous, discreet spirit and groundbreaking work as a theater director have propelled me down new paths of artistic and human discovery.

Dr. Evelyne Albrecht Schwaber wrote an early, brilliant commentary on a small piece of this book, which continues to inspire me, as do her psychoanalytic work and her profession in general.

Linda Nochlin cheered me on, always proud of her own family's support of the Spanish Civil War and tickled that her old art-historian pal was drawn to it as well.

My friend Chantal Maillet, another psychoanalyst and passionate cultural observer, was my European memory bank. Her aunt had joined the International Brigades as a Communist from France.

Patricia Grossman and Susan J. Miller are two friends whose writing and lives, unbeknownst to them, gave me courage.

I want to thank all the men and women who generously shared their memories of Dave with me in letters, in e-mails, over the telephone, and sometimes in person in extensive interviews. They are members of the Lipton/Lifshitz/Slavin family: Philip Lipton, Debbie Lipton, Louis Lipton, David R. Lipton, Trudy Lipton, Jack Slavin, and Ben Slavin; New York City friends and comrades of Dave: Ed Meskin, Bob Schrank, Adolph Ross, Herman Chermak, Quincy Goldberg, Rose (Morrison) Green, and Morris Schappes; and companions in Spain: Bill Wheeler, Bill Susman, Harry Fisher, Milt Wolff, Morris Stamm, Max Shufer, John Murra, Jack Shafran, Norman Berkowitz, and Ed Lending.

The Puffin Foundation and Mr. Jesse Crawford provided me with financial support that made a large difference.

I am deeply indebted to W. Clark Whitehorn, executive editor at the University of New Mexico Press, for his wholehearted enthusiasm for *A Distant Heartbeat*'s story and players. And I thank Grace Labatt for her imaginative, fastidious, and sensitive editing.

I could never do without the humor, edginess, smarts, and love of Kay Holmes. Stuart Jeffries kept coming up with contacts and sources I needed. I counted on his intelligence and critical faculty and directness.

Muriel Boselli's charm, skepticism, love, and breathtaking memory have meant an enormous amount to me. And Ed Alcock was always right there asking me his preternaturally dubious questions.

Lisa Lenz, analyst extraordinaire, what more can I say?

And thank you to my husband, Ken Aptekar, my dearest friend and critic.

Notes

14   "We wanted to reflect": "The Revolution Betrayed: An Interview with Ken Loach," by Richard Porton, *Cineaste*, Winter 1996, 30.

18   *Liberty Leading the People*: Painted in 1830, located in the Louvre.

37   *I decide to take*: The Abraham Lincoln Brigade Archive was moved in 2000 from Brandeis University to New York University's Tamiment Library and Robert F. Wagner Labor Archives.

38   *Perhaps I will be able*: As David Grossman so memorably put it, "Stalin once said, 'One death is a tragedy, a million deaths is a statistic.' When I read the stories of Bruno Schulz, I can feel in them—and in myself—the ceaseless pounding of an impulse to defy that statement, an impulse to *rescue* the life of the individual, his only precious, tragic life, from that 'statistic.'" David Grossman, "The Age of Genius: The Legend of Bruno Schulz," *New Yorker*, June 8–15, 2009, 70.

39   "who no more": Sigmund Freud, *Introductory Lectures to Psychoanalysis* (Harmondsworth, UK: Penguin Books, 1991), 42.

40   *I've been fascinated*: See Elaine Pagels, *The Gnostic Gospels* (New York: Random House, 1979); Elaine Pagels and Karen L. King, *Reading Judas: The Gospel of Judas and the Shaping of Christianity* (New York: Viking, 2007); and Karen L. King, *The Gospel of Mary of Magdala: Jesus and the First Woman Apostle* (Santa Rosa, CA: Polebridge Press, 2003). Even Dan Brown's *The Da Vinci Code* (New York: Random House, 2003)

and, perhaps most especially, its popularity are part of this dramatic rethinking.

41   "Hats twirling, armor flying": Jacqueline Osherow, "Views of *La Leggenda della Vera Croce*," in *Dead Men's Praise* (New York: Grove Press, 1999), 5, 6–7, 18.

43   "felt so warm": Canute Frankson in Cary Nelson and Jefferson Hendricks, *Madrid 1937: Letters of the Abraham Lincoln Brigade from the Spanish War* (New York: Routledge, 1996), 132.

43   "I saw in the invaders": Eluard Luchelle McDaniels in Peter N. Carroll, *The Odyssey of the Abraham Lincoln Brigade: Americans in the Spanish Civil War* (Stanford, CA: Stanford University Press, 1994), 18.

47   "Hi. Mind if I": I have invented the dialogue of the following pages, based on my sense of who Dave was and who Bill was and how Bill perceived Dave, as well as on details Bill communicated to me about their meeting on board.

53   "From the beginning": Robert Colodny in Alvah Bessie and Albert Prago, eds., *Our Fight: Writings by Veterans of the Abraham Lincoln Brigade* (New York: Monthly Review Press, 1987), 29.

57   "I knew your uncle": Quotes from people in this book are taken from correspondence, telephone calls, and taped conversations.

59   "In some cities": Fraser Ottanelli, *The Communist Party of the United States: From the Depression to World War II* (New Brunswick, NJ: Rutgers University Press, 1991), 29.

61   "Airplanes? Where'd you": Although the name is fictitious, "Mike" was a real person who contacted me after he saw an article I had written for the Veterans of the Abraham Lincoln Brigade magazine, the *Volunteer*, about my uncle, entitled "Tracking a Ghost," Winter 1996–1997, 16–17.

62   the *Good Fight*: *The Good Fight* is also the name of a 1984 documentary film with the subtitle *The Abraham Lincoln Brigade in the Spanish Civil War*, produced and directed by Noel Buckner, Mary Dore, and Sam Sills (Brookline, MA, and Brooklyn, NY: Abraham Lincoln Brigade Film Project).

64   "Dave was gentle": I spoke with Bob Schrank several times by telephone in the fall and winter of 1996–1997, and the words I attribute to him are taken verbatim from our talks. In his memoir, *Wasn't That a*

Time? Growing Up Radical and Red in America (Cambridge, MA: MIT Press, 1998), his descriptions of my uncle are briefer than they were in our discussions.

69   "At YCL headquarters": Schrank, *Wasn't That a Time?*, 169.

71   "middle class, filled with": Howard Fast, *Being Red: A Memoir* (Armonk, NY: M. E. Sharpe, 1994), 44.

74   "hotels in the Catskills": Ken Simon, "A Typical Day at Banner Lodge," SimonPure Productions, http://www.simonpure.com/resorts_banner01.htm.

80   "When [she] worried": Irving Howe, *The World of Our Fathers* (New York: Harcourt Brace Jovanovich, 1976), 177.

80   "A new heart's being born": Maxim Gorky, *Mother*, trans. Margaret Wettlin, illus. Kukryniksy, reprint ed. (1906; repr., Moscow: Foreign Languages Publishing House, n.d.), 137.

80   "Same old story": Isaac Babel, *1920 Diary*, ed. Carol J. Avins, trans. H. T. Willetts (New Haven, CT, and London: Yale University Press, 2002), 12, 28.

84   "remade the family": Vivian Gornick, *The Romance of American Communism* (New York: Basic Books, 1977), 8.

94   *words like "progressive"*: Ottanelli, *Communist Party*, 127.

95   *A party slogan*: Ibid., 123.

95   "We were an army": Steve Nelson in Noel Buckner, Mary Dore, and Sam Sills, prod. and dir., *The Good Fight: The Abraham Lincoln Brigade in the Spanish Civil War* (1984).

95   "We were proud": Alvah Bessie, *Men in Battle: A Story of Americans in Spain* (New York: Charles Scribner's Sons, 1939; San Francisco: Chandler & Sharp Publishers, 1975), 82. Citations refer to the Chandler & Sharp edition.

95   "I with other American": Ben Gardner in Nelson and Hendricks, *Madrid 1937*, 65–66.

95   "the hard core": Robert Colodny in Bessie and Prago, *Our Fight*, 28.

96   *the George Washington*: In February 1937, the American volunteers in Spain named themselves the Abraham Lincoln Battalion and were incorporated into the 15th International Brigade. In June, other American volunteers formed a second battalion, the George Washington Battalion. After the war, they became incorrectly known as the

Abraham Lincoln Brigade. "Brigade" is a misnomer, as a brigade consisted of four to six battalions.

96   "most of the volunteers": Carroll, *Odyssey of the Abraham Lincoln Brigade*, 16.

96   "They told me they had": Both quotes in Carroll, *Odyssey of the Abraham Lincoln Brigade*, 69.

96   "I felt I *had* to go": Ibid., 69.

97   "was politicized my": Ibid., 202.

97   "I only cared": Buckner, Dore, and Sills, *Good Fight*.

97   "Together with their": Hyman Katz in Nelson and Hendricks, *Madrid 1937*, 32, 34, 39.

97   "I can't live": Peter Frye to Judith Montell in Montell's *Forever Activists: Stories from the Veterans of the Abraham Lincoln Brigade*, a documentary film about the American volunteers, produced in 1990 by Montell Associates in Berkeley, California. See more about Frye on the Abraham Lincoln Brigade Archives website: http://www.alba-valb.org/volunteers/peter-frye.

97   "On the battlefields": Canute Frankson in Nelson and Hendricks, *Madrid 1937*, 34.

98   "all of these things": Ibid., 39.

98   "We were radicalized": Montell, *Forever Activists*.

98   "We learned in Spain": Both statements are made in Montell, *Forever Activists*.

100   "The Vets hated war": Fisher undoubtedly meant David Reiss, a battalion commander killed in 1938 by a direct artillery hit on headquarters.

100   "If it is any comfort": James Lardner in Nelson and Hendricks, *Madrid 1937*, 46.

100   *Colow, who was*: All quotes in the following two paragraphs are from Montell, *Forever Activists*.

101   "We marched and": Bessie, *Men in Battle*, 55–56.

101   "Yesterday the boys": Dr. John Simon in Nelson and Hendricks, *Madrid 1937*, 91–92.

102   "We were a bunch": Abe Osheroff in Buckner, Dore, and Sills, *Good Fight*.

102   "I began to think": Harry Fisher, *Comrades: Tales of a Brigadista in the Spanish Civil War* (Lincoln: University of Nebraska Press, 1998), 56.

102   "For six hours": Bessie, *Men in Battle*, 290–91.

102   "When I arrived": Montell, *Forever Activists*.

103   "Men went [to Spain]": Bessie, *Men in Battle*, 181–82.

103   "Just what it was": Edwin Rolfe in Nelson and Hendricks, *Madrid 1937*, 30.

105   *Psychologists still don't know*: This is precisely the subject of Louise Kaplan's remarkable book *No Voice Is Ever Wholly Lost* (New York: Simon & Schuster, 1996).

110   *Often we think that*: See Alicia Ostriker's poem "Sex Dream" for a representation of a mother's gracious desire for her young daughter to find the courage and leap onto a moving carousel. In the final lines, the mother describes herself as she watches her daughter: ". . . a woman / Who will bow, rise, and salute her / When she makes her move." Alicia Ostriker, "Sex Dream," in *The Imaginary Lover* (Pittsburgh: University of Pittsburgh Press, 1986), 29.

116   "raised questions . . . a suicide.": Carroll, *Odyssey of the Abraham Lincoln Brigade*, 257.

116   *VALB office*: Referring to the Veterans of the Abraham Lincoln Brigade office.

119   "They gave up": Dolores Ibarruri in Carroll, *Odyssey of the Abraham Lincoln Brigade*, 205, 367.

121   "Everybody knew where": Archie Brown in Nelson and Hendricks, *Madrid 1937*, 58.

122   "As the train ran along": Ibid., 59.

124   *habitual neglect by*: This has been somewhat corrected in recent years. See especially Julia Newman's documentary film *Into the Fire: American Women in the Spanish Civil War* (New York: Exemplary Films, 2002).

124   *Abe Osheroff musing*: All three statements are from Buckner, Dore, and Sills, *Good Fight*.

125   "What shook me up": Harry Fisher in Nelson and Hendricks, *Madrid 1937*, 114.

129   *When I was a girl*: Sholem Asch, *The Nazarene* (New York: G. P. Putnam's Sons, 1939).

130   "Milton Wolff, that twenty-three": Mary Rolfe in Nelson and Hendricks, *Madrid 1937*, 447.

130   *I read Wolff's novel*: Milton Wolff, *Another Hill: An Autobiographical Novel*,

with an introduction and afterword by Cary Nelson (Urbana: University of Illinois Press, 1994).

130 "hot baths—clean beds": Ibid., 283–84.

132 "You felt": Bessie, *Men in Battle*, 13.

132 "All along the road": Henry Eaton in Carroll, *Odyssey of the Abraham Lincoln Brigade*, 145.

133 "are magnificent": Joe Dallet in Nelson and Hendricks, *Madrid 1937*, 77.

133 "[m]ost wonderful place": Dr. John Simon in ibid., 87.

136 "that one can be": Albert Camus in Carroll, *Odyssey of the Abraham Lincoln Brigade*, 4.

137 "At any moment": Milt Wolff in Bessie, *Men in Battle*, 205–6.

137 "What is to guarantee": Ernest Hemingway, *For Whom the Bell Tolls*, reprint ed. (1941; repr., London: Arrow Books, 2004), 7.

137 "the wonderful feeling": Both statements are from Nelson and Hendricks, *Madrid 1937*, 65, 408.

138 "All the terrain": Archie Brown to Arthur H. Landis, *The Abraham Lincoln Brigade* (New York: Citadel Press, 1967), 551.

138 "For two and a half": Bessie, *Men in Battle*, 271–72, 289.

139 "All day and every": Hugh Thomas, *The Spanish Civil War* (New York: Harper & Row, 1977), 843.

140 *I have read*: Passim, Charlotte Delbo, *Auschwitz and After*, trans. Rosette C. Lamont (New Haven, CT: Yale University Press, 1997).

144 *Dave might have*: Nelson and Hendricks, *Madrid 1937*, 141.

144 "The actual fighting": Robert Hale Merriman in Nelson and Hendricks, *Madrid 1937*, 84. Merriman was a Californian who had been a teaching assistant in economics at the University of California, Berkeley, when he left for Spain.

145 "Yes [on the battlefield]": Bessie, *Men in Battle*, 291–92.

146 "I really don't think": Harry Fisher in Nelson and Hendricks, *Madrid 1937*, 187.

147 *by the window*: The *Morgen Freiheit*, a Yiddish-language newspaper, ran from 1922 to 1988 and was affiliated with the Communist Party until after the end of WWII.

Suggested Reading

The list below is a very particular selection of the most useful books, films, and archives I consulted for *A Distant Heartbeat*. They helped me both to understand the ethos of people's lives on the Left in 1930s New York and to reproduce the atmosphere among those politically committed men and women who fought and worked with the Abraham Lincoln Brigade in Spain. This list is not meant to be exhaustive. A few general histories of the Spanish Civil War are included as well.

Books

Bessie, Alvah. *Men in Battle: A Story of Americans in Spain*. San Francisco, CA: Chandler & Sharp Publishers, 1975. First published 1939.

Bessie, Alvah, and Albert Prago. *Our Fight: Writings by Veterans of the Abraham Lincoln Brigade, Spain 1936–39*. New York: Monthly Review Press, 1987.

Carroll, Peter N. *The Odyssey of the Abraham Lincoln Brigade: Americans in the Spanish Civil War*. Stanford, CA: Stanford University Press, 1994.

Carroll, Peter N., and James D. Fernandez, eds. *Facing Fascism: New York and the Spanish Civil War*. New York: New York University Press, 2007.

Carroll, Peter N., and Fraser Ottanelli, eds. *Letters from the Spanish Civil War: A U.S. Volunteer Writes Home*. Kent, OH: Kent State University Press, 2013.

Cohen, Robert. *When the Old Left Was Young: Student Radicals and America's First Mass Student Movement, 1929–1941.* New York: Oxford University Press, 1993.

Fisher, Harry. *Comrades: Tales of a Brigadista in the Spanish Civil War.* Lincoln: University of Nebraska Press, 1998.

Gornick, Vivian. *The Romance of American Communism.* New York: Basic Books, 1977.

Hemingway, Ernest. *For Whom the Bell Tolls.* New York: Charles Scribner's Sons, 1940.

Herman, Judith Lewis. *Trauma and Recovery.* New York: Basic Books, 1992.

Howe, Irving. *The World of Our Fathers.* New York: Harcourt Brace Jovanovich, 1976.

Kaplan, Louise J. *No Voice Is Ever Wholly Lost.* New York: Simon and Schuster, 1995.

Landis, Arthur H. *The Abraham Lincoln Brigade.* New York: Citadel Press, 1967.

Nelson, Cary, and Jefferson Hendricks. *Madrid 1937: Letters of the Abraham Lincoln Brigade from the Spanish Civil War.* New York: Routledge, 1996.

Neugass, James. *War Is Beautiful: An American Ambulance Driver in the Spanish Civil War.* Edited by Peter N. Carroll and Peter Glazer. New York: New Press, 2008.

Orwell, George. *Homage to Catalonia.* New York: Harcourt Brace Jovanovich, 1952. First published 1938.

Ottanelli, Fraser M. *The Communist Party of the United States: From the Depression to World War II.* New Brunswick, NJ: Rutgers University Press, 1991.

Preston, Paul. *The Spanish Civil War, 1936–39.* London: Weidenfeld and Nicolson, 1986.

———. *The Spanish Civil War: Reaction, Revolution, and Revenge.* New York: W. W. Norton, 2007.

Rolfe, Edwin. *The Lincoln Battalion: The Story of the Americans Who Fought in Spain in the International Brigades.* New York: Random House, 1939.

Thomas, Hugh. *The Spanish Civil War.* New York: Harper & Row, 1977.

Yates, James. *Mississippi to Madrid: Memoir of a Black American in the Abraham Lincoln Brigade.* Seattle, WA: Open Hand Publishing, 1988.

Films

Forever Activists: Stories from the Veterans of the Abraham Lincoln Brigade. Directed by Judith Montell. Berkeley, CA: Montell Associates, 1990.

The Good Fight: The Abraham Lincoln Brigade in the Spanish Civil War. Directed by Noel Buckner, Mary Dore, and Sam Sills. Brookline, MA, and Brooklyn, NY: Abraham Lincoln Brigade Film Project, 1984.

Into the Fire: American Women in the Spanish Civil War. Directed by Julia Newman. New York: Exemplary Films, 2002.

Land and Freedom. Directed by Ken Loach. London: PolyGram Filmed Entertainment, 1995.

Archives

Abraham Lincoln Brigade Archives. http://www.alba-valb.org.

Abraham Lincoln Brigade Archives at the Tamiment Library and Robert F. Wagner Labor Archives, New York University (formerly at Brandeis University). www.nyu.edu/library/bobst/research/tam.

Randall B. Smith Collection of Spanish Civil War Materials, Manuscripts and Archives Division, New York Public Library. http://www.nypl.org/sites/default/files/archivalcollections/pdf/smithrandall.pdf.